BEST OF

Amsterdam

Clay Lucas

Best of Amsterdam
3rd edition – January 2005
First published – July 2000

Published by Lonely Planet Publications Pty Ltd
ABN 36 005 607 983

Australia	Head Office, Locked Bag 1, Footscray, Vic 3011
	☎ 03 8379 8000 fax 03 8379 8111
	🖳 talk2us@lonelyplanet.com.au
USA	150 Linden St, Oakland, CA 94607
	☎ 510 893 8555 toll free 800 275 8555
	fax 510 893 8572
	🖳 info@lonelyplanet.com
UK	72–82 Rosebery Avenue, London EC1R 4RW
	☎ 020 7841 9000 fax 020 7841 9001
	🖳 go@lonelyplanet.co.uk

This title was commissioned in Lonely Planet's London office and produced by: **Commissioning Editor** Judith Bamber **Coordinating Editor** Adrienne Costanzo **Coordinating Cartographers** Amanda Sierp, Julie Sheridan, Chris Thomas **Layout Designer** Adam Bextream **Proofer** Jackey Coyle **Managing Cartographer** Mark Griffiths **Cover Designers** Gerilyn Attebery, Brendan Dempsey **Project Manager** Charles Rawlings-Way **Series Designer** Brendan Dempsey **Mapping Development** Paul Piaia **Regional Publishing Manager** Amanda Canning

Photographs by Lonely Planet Images, Martin Moos and Richard Nebeský except for the following: p17 Rick Gerharter/Lonely Planet Images, p44 Adina Tovy Amsel/Lonely Planet Images, p45 John Elk III/Lonely Planet Images, p46 Zaw Min Yu/Lonely Planet Images, p15 Gert Jan van Rooij/Stedelijk Museum. **Cover photograph** All lit up: night-time on Keizersgracht, Jon Davison/Lonely Planet Images. All images are copyright of the photographers unless otherwise indicated. Many of the images in this guide are available for licensing from Lonely Planet Images: 🖳 www.lonelyplanetimages.com.

ISBN 1 74059 685 4

Printed through The Bookmaker International Ltd
Printed in China

Acknowledgements Many thanks to the Stedelijk Museum for providing the image of the museum (p15)

HOW TO USE THIS BOOK

Colour-Coding & Maps

Each chapter has a colour code along the banner at the top of the page which is also used for text and symbols on maps (eg all venues reviewed in the Highlights chapter are orange on the maps). The fold-out maps inside the front and back covers are numbered from 1 to 6. All sights and venues in the text have map references: eg (3, C2) means Map 3, grid reference C2. See p128 for map symbols.

Prices

Multiple prices listed with reviews (eg €8/4) usually indicate adult/concession admission to a venue. Concession prices can include senior, student, member or coupon discounts. Meal cost and room-rate categories are listed at the start of the Eating and Sleeping chapters, respectively.

Text Symbols

☎	telephone
✉	address
🖳	email/website address
€	admission price
☯	opening hours
ⓘ	information
Ⓜ	metro
🚌	bus
🚋	tram
♿	wheelchair access
✗	on-site/nearby eatery
☗	child-friendly venue
Ⓥ	good vegetarian selection

Contents

From the Publisher

AUTHOR

Clay Lucas

Clay first crashed his bicycle on Amsterdam's cobbled streets in 1993, and has returned to this incredible city many times since to break countless Dutch cycling laws. He admires the good folk of Amsterdam for their offbeat sense of humour, their creative yet realistic solutions to social problems and their ability to be brutally frank. He had only two major bicycle collisions while researching this book.

Born the same year as Lonely Planet, Clay has worked as a newspaper sub-editor in Indonesia and Ireland, as a videotape editor, as one of the monkeys bashing away at keyboards for Lonely Planet's website, as a hack on several local newspapers, and has authored Lonely Planet guides to several European destinations. He lives in Melbourne.

Many thanks to Alex Klusman and the gorgeous young things at Booij en van Bruggen, Arwen Birch for the lessons in drinking at Cafe het Schuim, Evelyn Gebhart and Justine Dalla Riva for my birthday party, and Jan Lucas for all of her postcards.

The 2nd edition of this book was also written by Clay Lucas; Jeremy Gray & Nikki Hall wrote the 1st edition.

PHOTOGRAPHERS

Martin Moos

Born in Zürich, Switzerland, Martin got the obvious banking degree before escaping onto the travellers' trail with his Nikon gear in 1986. Seven years in Northeast Asia have provided oodles of motivation for an in-depth learning by doing. At present he is again based in Zürich, together with his wife and two children, hemmed in by mountains of slides.

Richard Nebeský

Richard was born one snowy night in the grungy Prague suburb of Žižkov but, surprisingly, he didn't have a camera in his hand. It was, however, not long after he got out of his cot that his father, an avid photo enthusiast, gave him his first point-and-shoot unit. Ever since, he's kept a camera by his side on treks, ski adventures, cycling trips and while researching Lonely Planet books around the globe. He has also worked for various magazines, travel guidebook publishers and on many social photography projects.

SEND US YOUR FEEDBACK

We love to hear from travellers – your comments keep us on our toes and help make our books better. Our well-travelled team reads every word on what you loved or loathed about this book. Although we cannot reply individually to postal submissions, we always guarantee that your feedback goes straight to the appropriate authors, in time for the next edition – and the most useful submissions are rewarded with a free book. To send us your updates – and find out about LP events, newsletters and travel news – visit our award-winning website: **www.lonelyplanet.com.**

Note: We may edit, reproduce and incorporate your comments in Lonely Planet products such as guidebooks, websites and digital products, so let us know if you don't want your comments reproduced or your name acknowledged. For a copy of our privacy policy visit www.lonelyplanet.com/privacy.

Introducing Amsterdam

The Dutch do things differently. Anyone requiring proof should come to Amsterdam. Countless visitors ask themselves the same question: 'Why can't my city be more like this?' But towns like this, with areas that should be up to 2m below water, don't come along often.

With its scenic, romantic canals, a peaceful city centre where bicycles and foot traffic hold sway, and a population below one million, Amsterdam isn't your standard urban dream factory. This offbeat metropolis is one of the world's great places to immerse yourself in world-class museums, cutting-edge galleries and the music of top-notch orchestras or live-jazz venues, in the head of several beers or a self-rolled smokestack. You'll find few grand monuments in Amsterdam – it's no Paris, New York or London. What you will find are the monumental achievements of a people whose entrepreneurial spirit and Calvinist work ethic made this famously progressive and utterly implausible place (with its 160 canals and 90 islands, all reclaimed from the sea) possible.

Amsterdam's original religious zeal may have faded, but the town's uniquely Dutch *gezellig* spirit has not. Loosely translated, *gezellig* (pronounced heh-*zel*-ick) describes kicking back, mellowing out and not getting hung up on someone else's preferences. In its early days, the city's people had to compromise and respect one another to achieve the epic task of keeping their town above water. This led to the flexibility for which the Dutch are famous and means new ways of thinking emerge first here: they had the world's first homosexual marriage and were the first to legalise euthanasia; their drug laws are the planet's most tolerant and their education system the most liberal.

Today, that same open-mindedness makes Amsterdam the perfect travel destination for punters of all persuasions.

Tiptoe through the tulips in a pair of Albert Cuypmarkt clogs

Neighbourhoods

Amsterdam might be small, but it punches well above its weight: its quirky neighbourhoods are a joy to explore, and its museums and art galleries hold untold riches.

At the heart of Amsterdam is **Centrum**. Just 1km long and 500m wide, it contains contrasts aplenty: red-light sleaze, wonderful bars and restaurants, the grandeur of Dam Square and the retail bustle of Kalverstraat and Nieuwendijk. **Nieuwmarkt** (east of Centrum) is known for its pubs and restaurants, while nearby **Waterlooplein** hosts a bustling market by day and some of Europe's best opera and ballet at the Stopera by night.

Waterlooplein segues into the landmark museums of the **Plantage**, and a few minutes northeast are the **Eastern Islands**, the elegant designer islands of KNSM and Java. Architecture and urban-design enthusiasts will love this area but, a 10-minute cycle further east, they'll go wild over the astounding **IJburg**, a major new residential district slowly rising from the sea on seven artificial islands.

Back in town at Muntplein, the city's busiest intersection, Centrum gives way to the **Southern Canal Belt**. Here Leidseplein and Rembrandtplein are the major cultural and nightlife centres. At the height of summer, both are choked with locals and tourists until dawn.

Follow the canals northwards and you'll come to one of Europe's top places to shop – the fashionable **Jordaan**. Some of the city's top restaurants, cafés and bars are here, too, and it draws a steady stream of young, beautiful and cashed-up locals.

Some of this same moneyed crowd has, in the last two years, headed for the multicultural **De Pijp** area. With the wonderful Albert Cuypmarket by day and great restaurants and bars at night, it's a great place to hang out.

> ## Off the Beaten Track
> If the major tourist sites are inundated or you'd just prefer to hang out with Amsterdam natives, try some of the lesser-known locales:
> - Sarphatipark, where De Pijp locals relax (p36)
> - the peaceful terrace of De IJsbreker, on the Amstel (p85)
> - the thronging Dappermarkt, with its cheap fruit and veg (p51)
> - the tranquil garden of the Willet-Holthuysen Museum (p26)

A laundry with a difference in the fashionable Jordaan area

Nearby to the northwest, visitors flock to the **Museumplein**, which has the Rijksmuseum on the northeast side and the Van Gogh Museum on the southwest side.

Nearby is **Oud Zuid**, with its elegant 19th-century streets and the wonderful Vondelpark, an oasis of green in the middle of the city.

Itineraries

Amsterdam is compact and its sights are many, so you can pack a lot into one day. Most attractions are within the canal belt, which takes less than 45 minutes to walk across. The best idea, if you really want to see a lot, is to rent a bicycle (see p114).

The most famous attractions (the Rijksmuseum, the Van Gogh Museum and especially the Anne Frank Huis) can get hopelessly crowded any time of year, though you can beat the crowds by going early in the morning or late in the afternoon (all three also open late one day a week, and are much quieter then).

The Museumjaarkaart gives free admission to many of the highlights listed below, and 400 other museums and galleries (see p116). If you'll be using public transport, get an Amsterdam Pass, which gets you into all of the big galleries and museums, and includes bus, tram and train journeys (see p113).

DAY ONE

Visit the Rijksmuseum or the Van Gogh Museum, and stroll the inner canals (the Singel, Herengracht, Keizersgracht and Prinsengracht). Spend time nursing a coffee or beer in the Jordaan district. Take in an art exhibition at the Oude Kerk, then wander the red-light district at night to see one country's re-markable attempt to regulate the world's oldest profession.

DAY TWO

Visit the Anne Frank Huis, then go to the colourful Albert Cuypmarkt. Wander back via Museumplein and down the beautiful Nieuwe Spiegel-straat, famous for its antique shops. Have a meal in the Southern Canal Belt, then a drink in Centrum.

Worst of Amsterdam
The bottom of the barrel in Amsterdam:
- Packs of drunken buck's-night revellers swarming through the red-light district
- The red-light district's equally annoying dealers
- The Heineken Experience
- Bicycle theft: 200,000 bikes get ripped off each year
- The stench of urine on Amsterdam streets
- The dragons that fall incandes-cently from a tangerine sky (when you overdo the magic mushrooms)

MARTIN MOOS

DAY THREE

Admire the creatures in the Artis Zoo, then go to the NEMO science museum on the waterfront. If it's warm, walk east to *Odessa*, a ship that has been refurbished to feature a groovy bar overlooking the docklands. Finish with some experimental dance at the Het Muziektheater.

Highlights

RIJKSMUSEUM   (3, C3)

Opened in 1885, the Rijksmuseum holds the Netherlands' largest collection of art and artefacts. And we are talking big here: the museum owns more than one million pieces, including Dutch paintings from the 1400s to the 1900s, 40 of which were done by Rembrandt.

INFORMATION
- ☎ 674 70 47
- 🖥 www.rijksmuseum.nl
- ✉ Jan Luijkenstraat 1
- € adult/those under 18 €9/free
- 🕑 9am-6pm
- ℹ free floor plan; audio tour (€4)
- 🚊 2, 5, 6, 7, 10
- ♿ good
- ✗ Cobra Café on Museumplein

Bike it to the Rijksmuseum

However, most of the Rijksmuseum is closed until 2008, as the gallery undergoes one of Europe's grandest makeovers at a cost of more than €200 million. But such is the embarrassment of riches held by Amsterdam's answer to the Louvre that even the pared-back Masterpieces highlights tour is unmissable.

Many will even feel that less is more when surveying the temporary 400-piece exhibition in the Philips wing. When it was in full operational mode, it was easy to get lost in the museum's huge collection. The Masterpieces exhibit cuts to the chase in no uncertain terms, by putting on display all of the most important and popular works, including Rembrandt's *Nightwatch*, Vermeer's *Kitchen Maid* and Frans Hals' *The Merry Drinker*. There are also plenty of other favourites, such as Delft pottery and the wondrous 17th- and 18th-century children's dollhouses.

The only downside to the smaller exhibit? The entire museum, when it was open, was gargantuan enough to absorb huge numbers. Not so the temporary museum: expect it to be hopelessly overcrowded unless you arrive early in the morning or late in the afternoon.

A One-Trick Pony?

In the 1900s, as Berlin, London and Paris competed to build the most imposing boulevards and the most majestic palaces, the wily Dutch were making do with just a few monumental masterpieces. The best of them is the Rijksmuseum, designed by Pierre Cuypers. The architect, though, could be accused of being a one-trick pony, since the building's whimsical façade (dating from 1885) bears a striking resemblance to that of Centraal Station, which Cuypers designed four years later.

VAN GOGH MUSEUM (3, B3)

When Vincent van Gogh killed himself in 1890, he was dirt poor, having sold only one painting in his lifetime. The paintings he left behind, though, made many others filthy rich. They also made him perhaps the world's most posthumously popular artist.

The Van Gogh Museum opened in 1973 to house the collection of Vincent's younger brother Theo. The museum holds many of the artist's most famous works, including the *Potato Eaters*, the *Yellow House in Arles*, the inevitable sunflowers, several self-portraits and his paintings inspired by Japanese prints. Van Gogh produced 1200 drawings and 900 paintings in his lifetime, and the museum owns 500 and 200 respectively, along with more than 700 letters.

INFORMATION
- ☎ 570 52 00
- 🖳 www.vangogh museum.nl
- ✉ Paulus Potterstraat 7
- € adult/those aged 13-17/child under 12 €9/2.50/free
- ⏰ 10am-6pm (to 9pm Fri)
- ℹ free floor plan; audio tour €1.50-4
- 🚊 2, 5
- ♿ good
- 🍽 gallery restaurant

RICHARD NEBESKY

The Life of Vincent

Vincent van Gogh (pronounced 'khokh', rhyming with the Scottish 'loch') was born in 1853 and had a short but amazingly productive life. Van Gogh died aged 37, but didn't pick up a paintbrush until he was 28. He produced most of his work in the final four years of his life, spent in France, where he shot himself to escape depression. Although Van Gogh sold only one painting in his lifetime, his work was to influence many later artists.

Kurokawa's elliptical exhibition wing

MARTIN MOOS

Most are displayed in the museum's Rietveld building, the base for the main collection. Van Gogh's paintings are on the 1st floor, his self-portraits are on the 2nd floor, and on the 3rd floor are works by his friends and contemporaries such as Gauguin, Monet, Toulouse-Lautrec and Pissarro.

Attached to the main building is the extremely successful temporary exhibition wing designed by Japanese architect Kisho Kurokawa. Commonly known as the Mussel, this ellipse-shaped building (most of it below ground level and facing a central courtyard) holds touring shows of both Van Gogh's work and that of his contemporaries.

Come early to avoid the crowds (after lunch, queues are as ludicrously long as at the Anne Frank Huis) or come on the wonderfully quiet Friday nights, when the museum is open until 9pm.

ANNE FRANKHUIS (5, C2)

More than 900,000 people a year cram into Amsterdam's most famous canal house and, with precious little space for visitors, this would rank among the city's lowlights but for its towering subject matter: the ordeal of a young girl who documented part of WWII's horror as no-one else did.

Anne Frank received a diary for her 13th birthday, three weeks before she went into hiding, and the attic in which she wrote that diary is the focus of this moving, often upsetting, place.

Anne's father Otto was a manufacturer who had the foresight to emigrate with his family from Frankfurt to Amsterdam in 1933. In December 1940 he bought the building that houses the Anne Frank Huis and moved his business there.

INFORMATION

- ☎ 556 71 05
- 💻 www.annefrank.nl
- ✉ Prinsengracht 267
- € adult/those aged
  10-17/under 10
  €7.50/3.50/free
- ⏱ 9am-9pm Apr-Aug,
  to 7pm Sep-Mar,
  closed Yom Kippur
- ℹ self-guided tour in
  English
- 🚊 6, 13, 14, 17
- ♿ good
- 🍴 museum café

By then the Germans had already tightened the noose around Amsterdam's Jewish population, and in July 1942 Otto and his wife and daughters, Anne (aged 13) and Margot (aged 16), went into hiding. The Frank family, along with the Van Daan family and a Mr Dussel, survived there until they were betrayed to the Gestapo in August 1944. No-one knows who betrayed them.

The Franks were among the last Jews to be deported from the Netherlands. Anne died of typhus in the Bergen-Belsen concentration camp in March 1945, a few weeks before it was liberated. Otto, the only member of the family to survive, published Anne's work. The *Diary of Anne Frank* has since been translated into 60 languages.

There is also a museum focusing on the persecution of Jews in WWII and the dangers of present-day racism. Avoid the lengthy queues and crowds (at all times of the year) by coming early in the morning or late at night.

Gifted Writer in the Making

Addressed to her fictitious friend, Kitty, Anne's diary traces the young teenager's journey through puberty and persecution and displays all the signs of a gifted writer in the making. It has been reissued in recent years complete with passages – originally deleted by her father – about her awakening sexuality and relationship problems with her mother.

JORDAAN (MAP 5)

The Jordaan (yoar-*darn*) neighbourhood was planned as a working-class district during Amsterdam's huge canal-belt project in the early 17th century. This was where the canal-diggers, bridge-builders, carpenters and stonemasons who built the upmarket Southern Canal Belt (see p14) lived. Today it's the city's most charming and relaxing area.

The name *Jordaan* is probably derived from the French *jardin* (garden), as many French Huguenots moved here to escape persecution in their native country. Before they arrived the area was full of market gardens. On the other hand, some historians contend that the name refers to the Bible's River Jordan.

INFORMATION

- 🖥 www.visitamster dam.nl
- ℹ️ VVV tourist offices (☎ 0900-400 40 40; per min €0.35)
- 🚋 13, 14, 17
- ♿ excellent

For centuries, Jordaan was a working-class area and a hive of rabble-rousers. This is hardly surprising given that by the early 1900s there was an average 1000 people per hectare (100m by 100m) living here. It was the first precinct where tarred roads replaced brick paving because the latter could be turned into barricades and projectiles during riots.

After WWI, new housing estates on the outskirts relieved congestion, and by the 1970s students, artists and well paid professionals were transforming the Jordaan into the yuppie stronghold it is today. But enough working-class and elderly people remain for it to retain some of its original charm, so take your time investigating its inviting pubs and restaurants, offbeat shops and weird little art galleries.

A Slippery Business

While it was still a canal, Lindengracht in Jordaan (pictured) was the scene of the Eel Riot, a ruckus provoked by the ancient folk game of eel pulling. The object of the game? To pull a dead eel off a rope strung over a canal while standing in a wobbly boat. It was banned in 1886. Later in the same year, the crowd at a Lindengracht street party defiantly ignored the law. The police got wind of it and duly arrived to pull down the rope. All hell broke loose, and when the smoke cleared, 25 people were dead and 120 wounded.

MARTIN MOOS

RED-LIGHT DISTRICT (2, D5)

Bikini-clad girls lit by lurid neon lights beckon wantonly, slimeball dealers push their wares, and sex shops display more pictures of penises entering all manner of orifices than you can poke a large dildo at. Sound like fun?

There's something oddly compelling about Amsterdam's throbbing red-light district, bounded by Warmoesstraat, Kloveniersburgwal and Oude Doelenstraat. It sucks in visitors, regardless of their moral stance, and it's a compulsion that's built the Amsterdam brand name the world over: everyone knows about Amsterdam and its liberal attitudes to sex.

INFORMATION

💻 www.pic-amsterdam .com

🚊 4, 9, 14, 16, 24, 25

♿ excellent

Seeing red in the red-light district

You needn't worry about your hormones staging a coup d'état on your brain here, though, because it's an oddly unerotic place. But it is fascinating.

The district's foundations were laid by the glories of the seafaring Dutch empire. When ships came in, this port city would get an injection of world-weary sailors with gold to splash about, and this is where women willing to soak it up were to be found.

These days, crowds clog the alleyways, peep shows and sex shops, while comely and not so comely maidens flaunt their wares – some while chatting absent-mindedly on their mobile phone, others with more concerted effort – from pink-lit windows to passers-by.

There are 450 windows in Amsterdam, and a street for every taste – Latinos on Oudezijds Achterburgwal and Molsteeg, Asians on Stoofstraat and the 'high-end' glamour pusses along tiny Trompetterssteeg by the Oude Kerk.

Despite the tawdry vibe, the red-light district is quite safe for tourists, and you're not likely to get mugged here – unless you try buying drugs from a street dealer or take photos of prostitutes or loiterers. However, if you're going to get pickpocketed in Amsterdam, this is the place.

A Bit of Amsterdam that Shall Remain Forever British

Only 5% of the women in the red-light district's 450-odd windows were born in the Netherlands; the majority come from the former Soviet Union and Eastern bloc countries. Most belong to the Red Thread (the prostitutes' union), and pay around €50 to €100 per day to rent their window, depending on its location. The average cost of a quickie? From €35 to €50 is normal for 15 minutes. And the percentage of business from British clients? An impressive 40%.

OUDE KERK (2, D4)

Standing like a lone bastion of piety amid the red-light district's sea of sleaze, the Oude Kerk is the most interesting of Amsterdam's big churches.

The city's oldest building and earliest parish church was built in 1306, and today represents one of Amsterdam's great moral contradictions: it is surrounded on all sides by women selling their bodies, gay and straight sex shops and live sex shows. Such is the church's architecture, though, that it seems to just sit there, thinking to itself, 'This too shall pass'.

Inside, as you gaze at its sturdy timber beams and intricately vaulted Gothic ceiling, you'll appreciate how much the city's founders achieved, building it when Amsterdam was little more than a village.

The church is dedicated to St Nicholas, the saint of water and protector of sailors, merchants, pawnbrokers and children (he was into multi-skilling). The folk of Amsterdam hoped St Nick would protect them from the waters of the IJ, which rose threateningly every time it rained. It wasn't water they needed protection from in 1452, when a great fire razed most of Amsterdam; miraculously, the church escaped undamaged though every building surrounding it perished.

Many famous locals lie buried under the church's worn tombstones, including Rembrandt's first wife, Saskia van Uylenburgh, who died in 1642 (Rembrandt himself lies in a pauper's grave in the Westerkerk; see p23).

The 47-bell carillon, installed in 1658, is considered one of the Netherlands' finest; it plays from 4pm on Saturdays.

The church is now as much an art gallery as a place of worship, with shows ranging from video installations and Aboriginal art to the brilliant World Press Photo exhibition, held for eight weeks from mid-April (p30).

INFORMATION
- ☎ 65 82 84
- 🖥 www.oudekerk.nl
- ✉ Oudekerksplein
- € €3
- 🕐 11am-5pm Mon-Sat, 1-5pm Sun
- ℹ free floor plan
- 🚃 4, 9, 16, 24, 25
- ♿ good

DON'T MISS
- Inscription above the bridal-chamber door that reads: Marry in haste, repent at leisure
- The church's stunning 1724 Müller organ
- The stained-glass windows from 1555
- The 15th-century carvings on the choir stalls, some of which are downright rude

At ease in sin city: the Oude Kerk

MARTIN MOOS

SOUTHERN CANAL BELT (MAP 3)

Amsterdam's centre is embraced by five circular waterways called the Grachtengordel (canal belt).

The three main waterways are the Herengracht (gentlemen's canal), Keizersgracht (emperor's canal, named after Holy Roman Emperor Maximilian I) and Prinsengracht (prince's canal, after the House of Orange).

INFORMATION
- 🖥 www.visitamster dam.nl
- ✉ bounded by Leidse-gracht, the Singel, Singelgracht and the Amstel
- 🚊 1, 2, 5, 13, 14, 17
- ♿ fair (footpaths can be narrow)

Spot the skinny buildings on Keizersgracht

All three canals were reserved for the houses of the wealthy, who ensured the authorities relaxed restrictions on the size of canalside plots. But taxes were levied according to the width of the property, so the gables shot up anyway, creating the beautiful landscape of tall, narrow and deep residences.

The distinctive canal architecture makes this a superb place for an extended stroll.

Along the Herengracht, the first of the three main outer canals to be built starting in 1670, the buildings are noticeably larger than those of the western Grachtengordel.

On what's known as the Golden Bend, on Herengracht between Leidsestraat and Vijzelstraat, sit the city's largest private mansions. Dutch architectural themes are still evident but the dominant styles are French: Louis XIV, XV and XVI. This remains A-grade property today, dominated by financial institutions and the swanky offices of doctors, lawyers and bankers.

South of Herengracht are the Keizersgracht and Prinsengracht. The houses here are less imposing but arguably less pretentious.

Playing Bridge

Amsterdam has 1281 bridges crossing its canals, and perhaps the most striking are those over the Reguliersgracht, the beautiful Canal of the Seven Bridges, cut in 1664. It's possible to count all seven when you stand on the Herengracht bridge. It's particularly special at night, when the bridges are lit up and their graceful curves reflect in the water.

STEDELIJK MUSEUM CS (4, A3)

While its Museumplein headquarters undergoes some much-needed renovations, the Stedelijk Museum has gone postal, moving temporarily into two floors of a former mail-distribution office building that's five minutes' walk from Centraal Station (hence the 'CS').

Stedelijk Museum means 'municipal museum', which is about as dowdy as a museum name can get. But this temporary museum's amazing collection is anything but dowdy. While in its classical but rather drab mansion on the Museumplein, next door to the Van Gogh Museum, the Stedelijk's brilliant collection of 20th-century art was beginning to look quite stale. The genius of the temporary move to this former office block has proved that the surrounds were making the paintings look a bit off-colour.

The 2nd floor (European art) and 3rd floor (post-WWII American art) of this sprawling former office block are a marvel, featuring many of the best paintings by some of the biggest names of the last century: Jackson Pollock, Kasimir Malevich, Piet Mondrian and Willem de Kooning, to name a few. There are also stunning displays devoted to Dutch architecture and design.

INFORMATION

- ☎ 573 29 11
- 🖥 www.stedelijk.nl in Dutch
- ✉ Oosterdokskade 5
- € €8/4
- 🕙 10am-6pm (to 9pm Thu)
- ℹ 573 27 37
- 🚆 22
- ♿ good
- 🍴 Eleven, on the 11th floor of the building

GERT JAN VAN ROOIJ

Stedelijk Museum CS, in the Post CS building

Renovations at the Museumplein headquarters – the first serious revamp in 110 years – won't be finished until 2007, so you've got a good few years to enjoy the temporary museum.

The museum also has a cutting-edge gallery, Stedelijk Museum Bureau Amsterdam, in the centre of Amsterdam, which supports young and emerging artists (see p30 for details).

This One Goes to Eleven
A visit to the gallery is not complete without a drink in Eleven, the wonderful new addition to Amsterdam's food and bar scene (see p86), which on Thursday nights will be the place to come for artist talks and screenings of films by or about artists; at the time of writing the details were still to be decided, so ring ahead.

AMSTERDAMS HISTORISCH MUSEUM (2, B6)

Understanding how Amsterdam transformed itself from a fishing village on the banks of a stagnant swamp to a bustling metropolis will make walking around town much more interesting.

A visit to the Amsterdams Historisch Museum will reveal just how implausible it was that this town ever came to be built in an age without electric pumps, bulldozers or mosquito repellent.

Housed in a labyrinthine monastery building dating from the

INFORMATION
- ☎ 523 18 22
- 🖥 www.ahm.nl
- ✉ Nieuwezijds Voorburgwal 357
- € €6/3
- 🕐 10am-5pm Mon-Fri, 11am-5pm Sat & Sun
- ℹ free guidebook
- 🚃 1, 2, 4, 5, 9, 14, 16, 24, 25
- ♿ excellent
- ✕ David & Goliath café

17th century, the museum begins with a slick computer-generated aerial map of Amsterdam showing how the city grew from AD 1000 until today. You then take yourself on a three-part tour of the city's history, divided into the years 1350–1550, 1550–1815 and 1815–2000. All three periods are well organised and packed with quirky displays (such as that on corset styles in 1930s Amsterdam, or the history of bicycle riding here). If that all sounds like too much to take in, you can opt for a much shorter highlights tour.

The city's fate during WWII is also well documented, with a brutally honest analysis of how the people of Amsterdam ('Heroic, Decided, Merciful', according to the city's coat of arms) defied, collaborated or coped with Nazi rule during the war. Another highlight is an objective look at drug use in the city and the development of coffeeshops.

By the time you leave, you'll realise what an astounding place Amsterdam is and how fitting it is that there be such a wonderful museum to eulogise it.

DON'T MISS
- Cornelius Anthoniszoon's 1538 painting *Bird's-Eye View of Amsterdam*
- The bell room
- The 700-year-old shoes, uncovered on an archaeological dig
- Café 't Mandje, Amsterdam's first lesbian bar

MARTIN MOOS

The lesbian Café 't Mandje, making history

IJBURG (1, F4)

Anyone with even a passing interest in design, town planning and urban growth needs to see how the good folk of Amsterdam go about building a new town.

When it is finished in 2012, the amazing seven isles that make up IJburg will be the place for 45,000 new residents living in around 18,000 new homes. There will be 11 new primary schools and even a cemetery, perhaps to give residents the comfort of knowing they can go from cradle to grave without ever having to leave the isles.

The IJmeer is the lake upon which Amsterdam is set, and in 1965, town planners and architects came up with an idea for a new city in the lake, adjacent to Amsterdam. Three decades later, in the 1990s, the City of Amsterdam took steps to make their dream come about, building a series of seven artificial islands of dredged sand.

However, it took the people of Amsterdam some convincing before the project got the nod. After the city council decreed the project would go ahead in 1996, an outburst from objectors led to a referendum in 1997. A huge majority voted against the isle being built, but not enough Amsterdammers voted, so the project got the go-ahead.

The first building on the islands was opened in 2001, and by 2004 there were a few hundred people already living out on the islands – a bit like the American pioneers of old, but with better coffee.

The new district has a bus line running to it, but the much-awaited IJ tram was due to open in late 2004, so bigger changes are imminent.

Breezing past IJburg

> ### INFORMATION
> - 🖳 www.ijburg.nl (in Dutch)
> - ⓘ guide map, available from Arcam (p29)
> - 🚊 IJburg tram from Centraal Station
> - 🚌 326
> - ♿ good
> - 🍴 Blijburg An Zee (see below)

Surf's Up

In 2003, Amsterdam became a beach city. At the eastern end of Haveneiland, the largest of IJburg's isles, is Blijburg, roughly 300 metres of sand, sea and sun cream. Thousands of trendy Amsterdammers pack this patch of beach on a hot day; on weekends, every way-gone hep cat and his or her dog heads there, and it can be a real sight, to see beautiful men and women battling it out for their little patch of beach. There's even a great bar, **Blijburg An Zee** (☎ 416 03 30; www .blijburg.nl; 🕙 closed Tue), which has snacks, expensive (and mediocre) meals and, most importantly, plenty of good beach booze.

VONDELPARK (3, A3)

On a sunny day, a party atmosphere descends on the wonderful Vondelpark, Amsterdam's sprawling equivalent to New York's Central Park.

INFORMATION

- ☎ 523 77 90 (theatre & concert info); 589 14 00 (Filmmuseum)
- 🖳 www.vondelpark.nl
- ✉ Stadhouderskade
- € free
- 🕑 24hr
- 🚊 2, 3, 5, 12
- ♿ excellent
- ✗ Café Vertigo at the Filmmuseum (p88)

Laid out as a green belt for the city's bourgeoisie in the 1860s and named after Holland's Shakespeare, poet and playwright Joost van den Vondel (1587–1679), the elongated park (300m by 1500m) offers a wealth of ponds, lawns, thickets and winding footpaths to while away the hours.

True to the great Dutch entrepreneurial spirit, the city financed the Vondelpark by reclaiming far more land than was needed and then selling the land surrounding the new park to developers – on the condition that no factories or workers' cottages be built. Thus sprung up Oud Zuid (Old South), one of Amsterdam's swankiest and most exclusive neighbourhoods.

The park is a mecca for joggers, Frisbee throwers, couples in love, families with prams and kids playing football. Film buffs gather at the Nederlands Filmmuseum (see p88), where free screenings are held in summer. Kids are free to frolic in several play areas alongside the tiny canal network, and southwest of Huygenstraat (which cuts through the park) is a petting zoo with goats, sheep and even a few llamas. Also at this end sprawls a fragrant rose garden (a popular gay sunbathing spot by day, a popular spot for cruising by night).

Summer sees free concerts in the open-air theatre, and there are always musicians, mime artists, jugglers and comedians performing in the park.

Round off an afternoon in the Vondelpark with a visit to the Round Blue Teahouse

Better Long Haired than Short-Sighted

In 1967, word spread that Amsterdam had tuned in and turned on, and hordes of hippies descended on the Vondelpark to drop out. The park soon became famous worldwide as an open-air dormitory for those seeking an alternative way of life, and for others who just wanted soft drugs and free love, baby. Many took as their catch cry 'Better Long Haired than Short-Sighted'. The sleeping bags might be long gone, as it's now illegal to sleep in the park, but on a sunny afternoon you'll still find plenty of '60s-inspired hippie types.

KONINKLIJK PALEIS (2, B5)

The sombre façade of the Koninklijk Paleis (Royal Palace) belies a lavish interior that only Golden Age Amsterdam could have produced. Completed in 1662, it was built as the town hall of the world's then most important trading city, and in its every extraordinary detail strived to show Amsterdam's power, wealth and wisdom.

The town hall served as a palace for a people who had prospered without kings and queens, showing that Amsterdam had no need for royalty's patronising benevolence.

Architect and painter Jacob van Campen, who was heavily influenced by Italian classicism, spared no expense. Due to Amsterdam's shifting soil, Van Campen built the town hall on 13,659 wooden pilings, a number still recited by Dutch school children. The richly decorated Civic Hall is a sea of sumptuous marble adorned with allegories of Dutch might and symbols of state. Above the Magistrate's Court entrance, for example, are two huge carved

INFORMATION

- ☎ 624 86 98
- 🖳 www.kon-paleis
  amsterdam.nl
- ✉ Dam Square
- € €4.50/3.60
- ⊙ times vary year
  round; ring to check
- ⓘ free guided tour
  2pm Wed
- 🚊 4, 9, 14, 16, 24, 25
- ⅙ excellent
- ✕ Grand Hotel
  Krasnapolsky
  café (p100); Villa
  Zeezicht (p77)

figures: a skeletal *Death*, holding an hourglass, and *Justice*, with his many instruments of torture. Hundreds of other carvings show explicitly the grotesque fate that befell those who betrayed Amsterdam.

In 1808, Napoleon Bonaparte's brother Louis was crowned king of Holland and given the town hall as a temporary palace; it has remained thus ever since (the town hall moved, for a time, to what's now The Grand, see p100). The building was handed down among royalty until in 1935, when the Dutch government bought and restored it for state functions.

The palace is now Queen Beatrix's official residence (she's a mere tenant, paying €0.50 rent a year), though she lives in The Hague and is only here for affairs of state.

DON'T MISS

- Poor old *Atlas*, on the outside of the rear of the palace, who for four centuries has held a 1-tonne copper ball on his shoulders
- The carvings of rats about the Bankruptcy Room
- The relief of a dog guarding his dead master above the Secretariat doors

Guess who?

ARTIS ZOO (4, C6)

Artis Zoo, the oldest on the European mainland and the world's third oldest, is the place to bring children in Amsterdam. Laid out in the former Plantage gardens, its lush surrounds are a delight to stroll around.

The zoo was founded in 1838 by an association called Natura Artis Magistra (Latin for 'Nature is the master of art') who aimed to link nature and art. It has around 8000 animals and an impressive planetarium and aquarium. The zoo grounds, with ponds and plant-lined winding paths, also serve as important botanical gardens; in spring when the flowers bloom, it's a riot of colour.

> **INFORMATION**
> ☎ 523 34 00
> 🖥 www.artis.nl
> ✉ Plantage Kerklaan 38-40
> € €14.50/11
> ⏱ 9am-6pm (to 5pm in winter)
> ℹ layout maps
> 🚊 6, 9, 14
> ♿ excellent
> ✕ Twee Cheetahs, overlooking the African savanna

Besides the usual zoo attractions – big cats, apes and gorillas, huge fish in tanks and the like – there's an African savanna where zebras, gazelles and other African species roam a couple of islands in a bird-filled artificial marsh. Duck into the special viewing pit and see the beasties up close.

The aquarium is another highlight. Built in 1882 and renovated in the late 1990s, the graceful purpose-built hall has almost 2000 fish. One tank shows a cross-section of an Amsterdam canal, complete with sunken bicycle corpses and eels. The tanks are enormous and the variety of colourful fish stunning, though it's a popular school outing and the joyful squeals inside can be deafening.

There is also a children's zoo where kids can pet ponies, calves and other cuddly critters. Daily animal feeding times include: birds of prey (11am), seals (11.30am and 3.45pm), crocodiles (2.30pm, Sunday only), penguins (3.30pm) and lions and tigers (3pm, daily except Friday). The planetarium has shows in Dutch every hour (from 10am, final show starts 4pm); English summaries are available from the ticket desk.

DON'T MISS
- The zoo's indoor rainforest
- The brutal crocodile feeding, each Sunday at 2.30pm
- The children's playground
- The butterfly house

MARTIN MOOS

All creatures slimy and slippery

BEGIJNHOF (2, B7)

Hidden behind the north side of Spui square (simply known as the Spui) is the secluded Begijnhof, one of many such *hofjes* (little courtyards) in Amsterdam. This tranquil place is surrounded by a former convent dating from the early 14th century.

With tiny gabled houses grouped around the well-kept courtyard, it's an oasis of peace in the middle of the city.

The Begijnhof was originally home to the Beguines, a religious sisterhood of unwed women from wealthy families who had taken vows of chastity. The last member of the community died in 1971.

In a bloodless coup in 1587, Calvinists confiscated all property belonging to the city. Unlike most others, the Beguines owned their homes and managed to retain them. Their Gothic church at the southern end of the courtyard, however, was taken from them and they resorted to the 'clandestine' church opposite (note the dogleg entrance).

The Gothic church was eventually rented out to the local community of English and Scottish Presbyterian refugees (among whom were America's Pilgrims) and still serves as the city's Presbyterian church. Some of the pulpit panels were designed by a young Piet Mondrian.

INFORMATION
- ✉ Spui, north side
- € free
- ☻ 8am–1pm
- ℹ VVV tourist offices (☎ 0900-400 40 40; per min €0.35)
- 🚋 1, 2, 5
- ♿ excellent
- 🍴 Caffè Esprit (p68)

Holding up: the Houten Huis (see below)

This is one of the few *hofjes* where the public is still welcome. Tour groups aren't allowed, and bicycles must be locked up outside. Other *hofjes* in Amsterdam previously open to the public have in recent years been made resident-only, and even the Begijnhof has curtailed its opening hours. To ensure it stays open, keep quiet and don't take any photos, as requested.

The Good Wood

The Houten Huis (wooden house) at No 34 in the Begijnhof is the Netherlands' oldest still-maintained wooden house, dating from 1465. To prevent houses subsiding on the muddy Amsterdam soil, most were once built of wood, to keep weight to a minimum. But in 1669, after disastrous fires, the city banned the construction of wooden homes. The heavier brick and stone houses that followed demanded foundation laid upon huge numbers of wood pilings, driven 11 metres into the ground. Many larger office and apartment towers rest on pilings (concrete replaced wood in the 1940s) that go as far as 60 metres down.

TROPENMUSEUM (4, C6)

Unless you really overdo the hash cookies, there's only one place in Amsterdam where you can stroll through a Javanese house, ramble along a noisy Arab street or narrowly escape a thunderstorm in the African savanna: the extraordinary Tropenmuseum (Museum of the Tropics).

INFORMATION

- ☎ 568 82 15
- 🖥 www.kit.nl
- ✉ Linnaeusstraat 2
- € adult/child 6-17/under 6 €7.50/3.75/free
- 🕙 10am-5pm
- ℹ free floor plan
- 🚊 9, 10, 14
- ♿ good
- ✕ grab a herring snack at the nearby Dappermarkt (p51)

The Tropenmuseum was started in the 19th century when a collection of objects from the colonies was formed for the 'amusement of the Dutch people'. Upon these dubious colonial foundations, an extraordinary collection began, and in 1926 the vast palace that now houses the museum was built to eulogise the glories of the Dutch empire. It was also a new home for the esteemed Royal Institute of the Tropics, which now runs the museum and is a leading research body in tropical medicine and agriculture.

During the 1970s, the museum shrugged off its imperialist past and got into the groove of a more culturally aware era; the subsequent overhaul put in place the imaginatively presented display you see today. It affords a sensitive and responsible look at the economic and environmental problems confronting the developing world.

A three-storey central hall offers reconstructions of daily life in several tropical countries. Exhibitions focus on music, theatre, religion, crafts, trade and ecology.

There are many multimedia displays, including videos, slides and recordings, and some displays even give off aromas typical of places in Africa, India and China – from a spice vendor's stand to a hot, dusty road. It's a treat for the senses, even if ethnology isn't your thing.

DON'T MISS
- Indonesian gamelan orchestra
- Carved wooden boats from the Pacific
- Giant totem poles and masks
- The sounds and smells of India display

RICHARD NEBESKY

A touch of the tropics in the Tropenmuseum

WESTERKERK   (5, C2)

The highlight of a visit to the Westerkerk is its 85m-high tower, known as Langer Jan (Tall John) and open from April to September. Soaring graciously above the rooftops of the Western Canal Belt, the tower (topped by a gaudy golden crown, the symbol of Hapsburg Emperor Maximilian) affords wonderful views after an exhausting but well-rewarded 187-step climb.

INFORMATION

- ☎ church 624 77 66; tower 689 25 65
- 🖳 www.westerkerk.nl
- ✉ Prinsengracht 279
- € free; tower €5
- 🕙 church: 11am-3pm Mon-Fri &, Jul-Aug only, 11am-3pm Sat
- 🚌 13, 14, 17
- ♿ church good, tower none
- ✖ Spanjer en van Twist (p76)

The carillon inside the tower has the city's loudest, largest and heaviest bells (the main one weighs 7.5 tonnes) and plays for an hour each Tuesday from noon.

Originally built for the western canal gentry, the Westerkerk was the world's largest Protestant church when finished in 1631 (until St Paul's in London surpassed it in 1710). Designer Hendrick de Keyser – also architect of the Zuiderkerk (see p34) and Bartolotti House (see p30) – died before it was finished, though his son Pieter completed the construction.

Westerkerk's 29m-wide and 28m-high nave, the largest of any Dutch Protestant church, is covered by a wooden barrel vault, as the marshy ground precluded the use of heavy stone. The huge main organ (1686) bears some of the few decorations in the scant interior: panels of biblical scenes by Gerard de Lairesse.

Rembrandt, who died penniless and heartbroken in a workman's flat at nearby Rozengracht 184, was buried here in 1669 in an unmarked pauper's grave. No-one knows the grave's exact location, but he is commemorated by a memorial to his cherished son Titus, who died in 1668 and is also buried here.

Flowers are often left outside the church in memory of Anne Frank (see p10), who would listen to the church bells from her hiding place nearby.

The Homomonument

On Keizersgracht, next to the Westerkerk, stand the pink granite triangles of the Homomonument (5, C3), a memorial to homosexuals persecuted by the Nazis. During the German occupation, homosexuals were forced to wear a pink triangle. You might also see flowers, usually laid by those who've lost someone to AIDS.

VERZETSMUSEUM (4, B5)

On 10 May 1940, Nazi Germany marched into the Netherlands, the first time in 400 years the country had been occupied.

The Verzetsmuseum (Resistance Museum) provides a chilling account of the five years of Nazi occupation that followed, and tells the moving stories of those who dared resist the might of the German war machine. It also gives a frank assessment of why the Netherlands failed so abysmally to protect its Jewish citizens from German clutches (see the boxed text on p27). While there's a huge amount of information, the museum has a great overview for those in a hurry.

INFORMATION
- ☎ 620 25 35
- 🖳 www.verzets museum.org
- ✉ Plantage Kerklaan 61
- € €5/2.50
- 🕘 10am–5pm Tue–Fri, noon–5pm Sat–Mon
- 🚋 6, 9, 14
- ♿ good
- 🍴 Restaurant Plancius next door

The museum transports you back to the 1930s and '40s, using heart-wrenching personal documents and photographs – supplemented with video images, interactive computer displays and tape recordings (all in Dutch and English) – to tell of the horrific choices many Dutch people were forced to make.

The exhibits, including original items (false IDs, clandestine printing presses) and personal testimonies, reveal how much courage it took to actively resist the Germans, so ruthless and insidious that neighbours, friends and even family were often considered untrustworthy. It also looks at the small minority who collaborated with the Germans – an issue that has shamed the Netherlands ever since.

At several points, museum visitors are confronted by dilemmas and asked what decision they would make; it can be quite confronting deciding what you would have done had you been faced with the same circumstances.

There is also a changing schedule of temporary shows that focus on modern warfare and oppression. All in all, this is possibly Amsterdam's best museum and certainly its most moving.

Images of the Resistance at the Verzetsmuseum

MARTIN MOOS

The Bicycle Thieves

A reminder of how strongly the Netherlands still remembers German occupation during WWII can be seen at football matches between the two countries. Soon after kick-off, the chant goes up: 'Give us back our bikes, give us back our bikes', a reference to the thousands of bicycles stolen when the Germans evacuated Amsterdam in May 1945 – a bitter memory expressed with the characteristically quirky Dutch humour.

NEDERLANDS SCHEEPVAARTMUSEUM (4, C4)

The Dutch got rich sailing the high seas, and their relationship with water is fundamental to the national psyche. It follows then that they should have an impressive Scheepvaartmuseum (Maritime Museum).

Since 1973 the museum has been housed in the imposing Admiralty's Store building, where in the 17th century the East India Company (the VOC; Vereenigde Oost-Indische Compagnie) loaded their ships before embarking on the nine-month journey to Jakarta, the VOC's Indonesian base. The museum owns the world's best collection of shipping memorabilia, its only real competitor being London's National Maritime Museum.

INFORMATION

- ☎ 523 22 22
- 🖳 www.scheepvaart museum.nl
- ✉ Kattenburgerplein 1
- € €7.50/4
- 🕙 10am-5pm Tue-Sun (10am-5pm daily Jun-Aug)
- ⓘ museum guidebook in English
- 🚌 22, 32
- ♿ good
- ✕ museum restaurant

The collection isn't easy to navigate for those without Dutch language skills, as few translations are provided for the huge array of flags, maps and weapons. The vast collection of amazing ship models is still impressive, though. Pride of place (and no translation required) goes to the 700-tonne *Amsterdam* moored behind the museum, a replica of one of the VOC's largest ships (the original sank in 1749, taking 336 crew and passengers with it). Look out for the Dutch lion on the prow and the proud statues of Mercurius (God of Trade) and Neptune (God of the Sea) astern.

On the top floor, enjoy city views the way most landlubbers don't – through a periscope built into the rooftop. Or, if you're a real sea dog, watch an enthralling re-enactment of a trip to the East Indies in the film room.

Piece of Mind

Some countries honour their war heroes with vast mausoleums and statues. In the Netherlands, if one grisly display on level two of the Scheepvaartmuseum is anything to go by, they just scrape up the hero's exploded remains and slap them in a glass jar. Jan van Speyk was a Dutch lieutenant who in 1831, rather than lose a sea battle to the Belgians, blew his ship (and all his crew) sky-high by throwing his lit cigar into the ship's gunpowder store. Ever since, the Dutch have celebrated Van Speyk's patriotism and self-sacrifice.

Got cannons on the brain? Visit the Scheepvaartmuseum.

Sights & Activities

MUSEUMS

Allard Pierson Museum (2, C7)

The University of Amsterdam's wonderful collection of archaeological finds isn't quite in the same league as the Leiden collection (p46). But the exhibits (Egyptian, Mesopotamian, Roman and Greek, among others) are still captivating. Kids will love the models of Egyptian pyramids. ☎ 525 25 56 🖳 www .uba.uva.nl/apm ✉ Oude Turfmarkt 127 € €5/2.50 ☷ 10am-5pm Tue-Fri, 1-5pm Sat & Sun ☷ 4, 9, 14, 16, 24, 25 ♿ excellent

Bijbels Museum (2, A7)

There's nothing Holy Joe about the Bible Museum, with its confronting exhibitions questioning the role of religion in our times. Alongside temporary displays are wonderful rooms focusing on Middle Eastern and Egyptian archaeology, with models of biblical scenes that everyone's inner child will adore.

> ### Coffee Grounds
> In 1706 a Dutch merchant snuck a coffee plant out of Ethiopia and brought it to the Hortus Botanicus, making it the first coffee plant in Europe. The Dutch sent the plant to Brazil, which is now the world's greatest coffee producer.

☎ 624 24 36 🖳 www .bijbelsmuseum.nl ✉ Herengracht 366 € €6/3 ☷ 10am-5pm Mon-Sat ☷ 1, 2, 5 ♿ good

Hortus Botanicus (4, A5)

A garden of earthly delights for green thumbs, the Hortus Botanicus (Botanical Garden) opened in 1682 and became the repository for the Dutch empire's amazing tropical plant collection. Today the gardens, the monumental palm house and the modern three-climate glasshouse hold more than 8000 subtropical, tropical and desert plant species, and the world's oldest potted plant, a 300-year-old cycad.

☎ 625 84 11 🖳 www .hortus-botanicus.nl ✉ Plantage Middenlaan 2 € €6/3 ☷ 9am-5pm Mon-Fri, 11am-5pm Sat & Sun (to 4pm Nov-Mar) ☷ 7, 9, 14 ♿ good

Houseboat Museum (5, C4)

You could bail up a local *woonboot* (houseboat) resident and demand a snoop round their pad. Or you could pay a visit to the *Hendrika Maria*, a very comfortable old houseboat built in 1914, to get a feel for life on the low seas. ☎ 427 07 50 🖳 www .houseboatmuseum.nl ✉ opposite Prinsengracht 296 € €3 ☷ 11am-5pm Wed-Sun Mar-Oct, to 5pm Fri-Sun Nov-Feb, closed Jan ☷ 13, 14, 17 ♿ fair

Joods Historisch Museum (2, F8)

A beautifully restored complex of four linked synagogues, the Jewish Historical Museum has an impressive collection, detailing the rise of Jewish enterprise and its role in the Dutch economy. The WWII section is as disturbing as you'd expect. ☎ 626 99 45 🖳 www .jhm.nl ✉ JD Meijerplein 2-4 € €6.50/4 ☷ 11am-5pm (closed Yom Kippur) ☷ 9, 14 ♿ good

Meek, mild-mannered house on the outside, full-blown clandestine church on the inside (Museum Amstelkring)

MARTIN MOOS

Museum Amstelkring (2, E4)

The house at Oudezijds Voorburgwal 40 looks like any other. But inside it's home to Our Lord in the Attic, an amazing church dedicated to St Nicholas. Built in 1661, it's one of several clandestine Catholic churches established after the Calvinists seized power in the 16th century, when Catholic church property was confiscated and Catholics were only allowed to worship on camouflaged, privately owned property.
☎ 624 66 04 🖳 www .museumamstelkring.nl ✉ Oudezijds Voorburgwal 40 € €7/5 🕑 10am-5pm Mon-Sat, 1-5pm Sun 🚊 4, 9, 16, 24, 25 ᵹ poor

Museum Van Loon (3, D2)

It must have been dandy to have been a rich canal-house resident in the 18th century. To appreciate just how dandy, visit Museum Van Loon, with its lavish Louis XVI interiors.
☎ 624 52 55 🖳 www .museumvanloon.nl ✉ Keizersgracht 672 € adult/student/child under 12 €5/4/free 🕑 11am-5pm Fri-Mon 🚊 16, 24, 25 ᵹ poor

Museum Willet-Holthuysen (2, D8)

Named after the millionaire's widow who bequeathed this monolithic mansion to the city in 1889, the Willet-Holthuysen is decorated in high-camp neo–Louis XVI style. The garden out the back is a grand place for a rest.

☎ 523 18 22 🖳 www .willetholthuysen.nl ✉ Herengracht 605 € €4/2 🕑 10am-5pm Mon-Fri, 11am-5pm Sat & Sun 🚊 4, 9, 14 ᵹ fair

Museumwerf 't Kromhout (4, D5)

Ahoy, boat lovers: this is the place to come for anyone who shares the Dutch love of vessels other than those used for beer. On an 18th-century wharf on the outer side of the dyke, boats are repaired in one of its halls, while another hall has a museum devoted to shipbuilding.
☎ 627 67 77 ✉ Hoogte Kadijk 147 € €5/3 🕑 10am-3pm Tue 🚊 9, 10, 14 ᵹ good

NEMO (4, B3)

Renzo Piano's striking building – resembling the bow of a huge green ship – houses a magnificent science museum that kids and adults alike will love. NEMO has completely given up on the old-style museum concept and gone for every bit of techno-wizardry it can get its hands on. See robots come to life or discover the magic of metal. The free rooftop plaza has panoramic views of Amsterdam.
☎ 531 32 33 🖳 www .e-nemo.nl ✉ Oosterdok 2 € adult/student/child under 4 €11/6/free 🕑 10am-5pm Tue-Sun (open Mon Jul-Aug) 🚌 22, 32 ᵹ excellent

The Demise of Jewish Amsterdam

In May 1940, Amsterdam's Jewish population was 80,000. By Liberation in May 1945, it was 5000. It's hard to determine if non-Jewish Amsterdam knew what was happening, because the Germans systematically uprooted, marginalised and isolated the Jewish community in a way that made its fate unclear to the rest of the populace. But what is clear is the number of German officers involved in shipping Amsterdam's Jews to Auschwitz and Bergen-Belsen: 60. The rest of the work was done by the Dutch.

Kosher kitchen supplies in the Joods Historisch Museum

Pianola Museum (5, C1)

All your life you've wanted to know more about the pianola. Here's your chance. This is quite a special place, with some 15,000 rolls of music for its many player pianos.

☎ 627 96 24 🖳 www .pianola.nl ✉ Wester-straat 106 € €4/2.50 🕑 11.30am-5.30pm Sun 🚋 3, 10 ⑤ fair

Rembrandthuis (2, E7)

This impressive 17th-century house is where Rembrandt van Rijn lived and worked at the height of his career. The museum owns over 250 of his etchings – 90% of his drawing output. Rembrandt bought the house in 1639, but chronic debt eventually forced him to move to a worker's flat, at Rozengracht 184 in the Jordaan area.

☎ 520 04 00 🖳 www .rembrandthuis.nl ✉ Jodenbreestraat 4 € €7/1.50 🕑 10am-5pm Mon-Sat, 1-5pm Sun 🚋 9, 14 ⑤ fair

Theatermuseum (2, A4)

Even if you're not a fan of Dutch theatre history this museum is well worth a visit for the dioramas, costumes, stunning interior, fantastic spiral staircase and magnificent frescoes. And don't miss the lovely garden in summer.

☎ 551 33 00 🖳 www .tin.nl ✉ Herengracht 168 € €4.50/2.25 🕑 11am-5pm Mon-Fri, 1-5pm Sat & Sun 🚋 13, 14, 17 ⑤ fair

Tram Museum (1, B4)

Tram spotters flock to this museum, in the beautiful

Is it a boat? Is it a plane? No, it's NEMO! (p27)

RICHARD NEBESKY

1916 Haarlemmermeer Station, to take a one-hour voyage on its glorious rolling stock – historic trams from all over Europe. The beautiful trams rattle through the nearby Amsterdamse Bos (p35). Ring ahead for opening times, as those listed are subject to change.

☎ 673 75 38 🖳 www .museumtram.nl in Dutch ✉ Haarlem-mermeer Station, Amstelveenseweg 264 € €4.50/2.25 🕑 11am-5pm Sun Apr-Jun & Sep, noon-5pm Wed Jul-Aug 🚋 16 ⑤ excellent

Cheap Sex

Too timid to peruse one of the city's sex shops? The wimps' option is a visit to the tawdry **Sexmuseum Amsterdam** (2, D3; ☎ 622 83 76; Damrak 18; admission €2.50; 🕑 10am-11.30pm). There are a few interesting titbits, including excerpts from early lewd flicks, the odd ivory dildo and Victorian porn sure to cause a snigger, but it all seems a bit tame compared to what you can view for free by perusing the racks of Amsterdam's many porn purveyors.

All too tame – the goddess of love at the Sexmuseum

MARTIN MOOS

GALLERIES

The Dutch love anything original, meaning a profound respect for the visual arts that is not so prominent in other cities. That they love to be at the bleeding edge of change also makes for some art that will mystify those not totally devoted to deconstructionism and Derrida. But as many of the smaller commercial galleries listed tend to be grouped together, you don't have to go far to find a gallery to your taste.

New galleries spring up all the time in Amsterdam. For up-to-date listings get the *Exhibitions Amsterdam* gallery list published every two months by **AKKA** (www.akka.nl). Most galleries have copies, as does the wonderful Artimo A-Z art bookshop on Elandsgracht (p55).

Annet Gelink Gallery (5, B4)
One of a batch of cutting-edge, classy commercial galleries in Jordaan, the hefty space and the light flooding into Annet Gelink's make it a great place to catch up on who's hot right now in the Dutch art world. ☎ 330 20 65 ⌨ www .annetgelink.com ✉ Laurierstraat 187-189 € free 🕒 11am-6pm Tue-Fri, 1-6pm Sat 🚊 7, 10, 13, 14, 17 ♿ good

Arcam (4, B4)
The Amsterdam Centre for Architecture lives the design-excellence dream, located in a wonderful silver-disk building on the waterfront opposite NEMO (p27). Arcam is dedicated to all things architectural, as well as the promotion of Dutch architecture. It has regularly changing exhibits on Amsterdam architecture and also organises tours and lectures. Design boffins will love it. ☎ 620 48 78 ⌨ www .arcam.nl ✉ Prins Hendrikkade 600 € free 🕒 1-5pm Tue-Sat 🚌 22, 32 ♿ excellent

CoBrA Museum (1, C6)
The influential CoBrA art movement, formed after WWII by Danish, Belgian and Dutch artists (CoBrA derives from the first letters of each country's capital city), is celebrated in this not-to-be-missed gallery, 30 minutes from the city centre by metro. Artists on show include Asger Jorn, Corneille and Karel Appel, and graphic-art star MC Escher. ☎ 547 50 50 ⌨ www .cobra-museum.nl ✉ Sandbergplein 1-3 € €7.50/3.50 🕒 11am-5pm Tue-Sun Ⓜ Amstelveen 🚌 bus 170, 172 ♿ good

De Appel (3, D1)
Nieuwe Spiegelstraat is crammed with antique shops, but this contemporary art space is anything but antique. It hosts a changing schedule of local and international painters, sculptors and multimedia artists. ☎ 622 56 51 ⌨ www .deappel.nl ✉ Nieuwe Spiegelstraat 10 € €2.50 🕒 11am-5pm Tue-Sun 🚊 1, 2, 5, 7, 10, 16, 24, 25 ♿ good

FOAM (3, D2)
The Fotografi Museum Amsterdam (FOAM), opened in 2003, and its functionalist exhibition space, which runs over two levels, has already

The AvAnT-gArDe CoBrA Museum of Modern Art

RICHARD NEBESKY

Flash photography at FOAM

seen some top-notch shows. Several world-renowned photographers are due to show here in 2005.
☎ 551 65 00 🖵 www .foam.nl ✉ Keizersgracht 609 € adult/child €5/free 🕒 10am-5pm Sat-Wed, to 9pm Thu & Fri 🚊 16, 24, 25 ♿ good

Galerie Fons Welter (5, B3)
Look for the strangely bulbous yet strangely cool

fibreglass doors out front of Fons Welter. Things stay just as slick inside this gallery, which consistently puts on great sculpture and installation shows by both emerging and mid-career artists.
☎ 423 30 46 ✉ Bloem-straat 140 € free 🕒 1-6pm Tue-Sat 🚊 13, 14, 17 ♿ good

Reflex Modern Art Gallery (3, C2)
Reflex was once a trend-setter among Amsterdam galleries. Now 15 years old, it's no longer the talk of the town, but still shows great Dutch and international art.
☎ 627 28 32 🖵 www .reflex-art.nl ✉ Weter-ingschans 79A € free 🕒 11am-6pm Tue-Sat 🚊 2, 5, 6, 7, 10 ♿ good

Stedelijk Museum Bureau Amsterdam (5, B3)
As well as its wonderful museum next to Centraal

Station (p15), the Stedelijk also runs this space dedi-cated to younger Dutch artists and some inter-national artists. A must-see for any contemporary art enthusiast.
☎ 422 04 71 🖵 www .smba.nl ✉ Rozenstraat 59 € free 🕒 11am-5pm Tue-Sun 🚊 13, 14, 17 ♿ poor

Stichting de Oude Kerk (2, D4)
Don't miss the World Press Photo show (www.world pressphoto.nl), staged for eight weeks each year at the Oude Kerk from mid-April. Other temporary exhibitions (eg on Aboriginal art), are held in this amazing church (p13) year round.
☎ 625 82 84 🖵 www.oudekerk.nl ✉ Oudekerksplein 23 € €4 🕒 11am-5pm Mon-Sat, 1-5pm Sun 🚊 4, 9, 16, 24, 25 ♿ good

NOTABLE BUILDINGS & MONUMENTS

ABN-AMRO Bank Building (3, D1)
This imposing pile was completed in 1923 as head office for the Netherlands Trading Society, the succes-sor to the United East India Company and West India Company.
✉ cnr Herengracht & Vijzelstraat € free 🚊 16, 24, 25 ♿ good

Bartolotti House (2, A4)
Next door to the Theater-museum, this lovely private residence, built in 1615, has one of Amsterdam's most

stunning façades: a red-brick Dutch Renaissance job that follows a bend in the canal.
✉ Herengracht 170-172 € free 🚊 13, 14, 17 ♿ good

Beurs van Berlage (2, D4)
Named after Dutch master architect HP Berlage, the former stock exchange (1903) is one of Amster-dam's most striking landmark buildings, with functional lines and a spartan clock tower. The large central hall, with its airy steel-and-glass roof,

was once the commodi-ties exchange. The traders eventually moved to the neoclassical Effectenbeurs (1913) on the eastern side of Beursplein. Berlage's Bourse is now a concert and cultural centre.
✉ Damrak 277 🚊 4, 9, 16, 24, 25 ♿ good

Centraal Station (2, E2)
In Dutch Renaissance style (1889) with Gothic elements, this edifice was built to a blueprint by Pierre Cuypers (who also designed the Rijksmuseum) and AL van

Gendt, the architect of the Concertgebouw (see below).
☎ 0900-42 42
✉ **Stationsplein 51**
€ free 🚋 1, 2, 4, 5, 9, 13, 16, 17, 24, 25
♿ excellent

Concertgebouw (3, B4)

Completed in 1888 to a neo-Renaissance blueprint by AL van Gendt (the ugly glass foyer on the south side was added in the 1980s), the Concertgebouw attracts 800,000 visitors per year, making it the world's busiest concert hall (see p92).
☎ 675 44 11 🖳 www .concertgebouw.nl
✉ **Concertgebouwplein 2-6** 🚋 3, 5, 12
♿ excellent

Dam Square & Nationaal Monument (2, C5)

This pigeon-filled expanse was the site of the original dam built across the Amstel that gives the city its name. Filled in 1672, it became the central market square. The obelisk at its eastern end is the Nationaal Monument,

built in 1956 to honour the fallen in WWII. The statues perched on it represent war, peace and resistance. Overlooking the square is the imposing Koninklijk Paleis (p19) on one side, and Bijenkorf department store on the other.
✉ **Dam Square** € free
🚋 4, 9, 16, 24, 25
♿ excellent

De Gooyer Windmill (4, E6)

A remnant of the 18th century, this former grain mill (1814) is the sole survivor of five windmills that once stood in this part of town. In 1985 the former public baths alongside were converted into a small brewery, the Bierbrouwerij 't IJ (p85).
☎ 622 83 25
✉ **Funenkade 7** € free
🕑 3-7.45pm Wed-Sun (brewery), tour 4pm Fri
🚋 9, 14 🚌 22, 32
♿ fair

De Waag (2, E5)

The imposing Weigh House started life on Dam Square in 1488 as one of three

gates in the huge city wall. It became a weigh house in 1617, Amsterdam having fallen upon peaceful times. In 1808 the newly crowned king of Holland, Louis Bonaparte, decided the weigh house on the Dam spoiled the view from his palace so he moved the entire weighing functions of the city here, along with all public executions.
☎ 422 77 72
✉ **Nieuwmarkt square**
€ free 🚋 4, 9, 16, 24, 25
Ⓜ **Nieuwmarkt**
♿ excellent

Engelse Kerk (2, B7)

The prim little Gothic English Reformed Church in the Begijnhof (p21) was originally Catholic, but today serves as the city's Presbyterian church, ministering mainly to British and Scottish expats. Its excellent acoustics lure lots of classical ensembles.
☎ 624 96 65 (concert ticket info) ✉ **Begijnhof 48** 🕑 11am-6pm 🚋 1, 2, 5, 13, 17 ♿ fair

From hippy hang-out to pigeon magnet: Nationaal Monument, Dam Square

Narrow-minded
Property in Amsterdam was once taxed on frontage – the narrower the house, the lower the tax. Hence there are a few extremely skinny specimens around town. Two of the narrowest are Oude Hoogstraat 22, east of Dam Square (2, D6), only 2.02m wide and 6m deep; and Singel 144 (2, B3), a mere 1.8m across the front, but widening to a generous 5m at the rear.

Greenpeace Building (5, C2)
It still gets called the Greenpeace Building, though they moved long ago. The building is a rare example of Art Nouveau architecture in Amsterdam.
☎ 422 33 44 ✉ Keizersgracht 174 € free ⛆ 13, 14, 17 🚌 21, 170, 171, 172 ♿ good

House on the Three Canals (2, C6)
This charming 1690 home at a pretty spot across from the university was previously owned by a succession of prominent Amsterdam families; it's now a student bookshop specialising in linguistic and literature titles.
✉ Oudezijds Achterburgwal 249 € free ⛆ 4, 9, 16, 24, 25 ♿ excellent

House with the Heads (2, A3)
One of the finest examples of Dutch Renaissance architecture, this house's beautiful step gable has six heads at door level representing the classical deities. But folklore has it that the heads are actually of burglars decapitated by an axe-wielding maid of the original owner.
✉ Keizersgracht 123 € free ⛆ 13, 14, 17 🚌 21, 170, 171, 172 ♿ excellent

In't Aepjen (2, E3)
At Zeedijk 1 you'll find Amsterdam's oldest bar, In't Aepjen, which translates as In the Monkeys. The building began life as a boozer for sailors in the 1500s; the barman was a generous fellow who allowed the seamen to pay their bar tab by handing over the monkey they'd brought back from the tropics. It's still a great place for a drink, even if you don't have your monkey on hand to settle the bill.
☎ 626 84 01 ✉ Zeedijk 1 € free Ⓜ Centraal Station ♿ good

Magere Brug (3, F2)
It means 'Skinny Bridge' but the name reputedly comes from the Mager sisters, who, three centuries ago, built a narrow footbridge to get to their vegetable garden. It's the most photographed drawbridge in the city.
✉ Kerkstraat on the River Amstel € free ⛆ 4, 9, 14 ♿ good

RICHARD NEBESKY

Greenpeace may be gone but the building stays on

Magna Plaza (2, B4)

Formerly the main post office, the Magna Plaza was built in 1899. The imposing orange-and-white pile has now been converted into a shopping centre dominated by clothing boutiques. It's worth popping inside just for the top-floor view of the interior grand hall.

✉ **Nieuwezijds Voorburgwal 182** € free
🚋 1, 2, 5, 13, 17
♿ excellent

Nationaal Vakbondsmuseum (4, B5)

The Trade Union Museum, former home of the powerful General Netherlands Diamond Workers' Union (one of the pioneers of the Dutch labour movement – perhaps that's why the turrets were necessary) was designed by architect HP Berlage in 1900. It's considered his most successful work.

☎ 624 11 66 ✉ **Henri Polaklaan 9** € €3/2
🕐 11am-5pm Tue-Fri
🚋 9, 14 ♿ fair

Nieuwe Kerk (2, B4)

The New Church is only new in relation to the Old Church (Oude Kerk, p13). Completed in 1408 after the Oude Kerk became too packed with prayerful parishioners, the late-Gothic church has an imposing presence on Dam Square's northwest corner. It has been the coronation church of Dutch monarchs since 1814; Queen Beatrix was crowned here in 1980. At the time of writing, it was undergoing renovations that were expected to be complete by late 2004.

Tower of Money

There's always been tension between moneymaking and worshipping the Almighty in Amsterdam. So, when the city burghers were beavering away on the town hall in the 1640s (p19), the clergy at the Nieuwe Kerk demanded that the church's tower be raised to far surpass the cupola of the town hall – to demonstrate God's supremacy over all. The burghers agreed and plans for raising the church's tower were drawn up. Tellingly, the new tower was never built.

The late-Gothic, not-so-new Nieuwe Kerk

☎ 638 69 09 🖥 www.nieuwekerk.nl ✉ **Dam Square** € €4 🕐 10am-6pm 🚋 1, 2, 4, 5, 9, 13, 14 ♿ good

Noorderkerk (2, A1)

Built in the shape of a broad Greek cross (four arms of equal length) around a central pulpit, the Noorderkerk boasts an unusual design for a Calvinist church of the time (1632). It's rarely open to the public.

☎ 624 78 19 ✉ **Noordermarkt** 🚋 1, 2, 5, 13, 17
♿ excellent

Oostindisch Huis (2, D6)

The impressive former headquarters of the mighty VOC (Vereenigde Oost-Indische Compagnie), the United East India Company, whose trade with the Far East once made the Netherlands exceedingly rich.

✉ **Kloveniersburgwal, cnr Oude Hoogstraat** € free 🚋 4, 9, 16, 24, 25 ♿ excellent

Portuguese-Israelite Synagogue (2, F7)

This majestic structure was Europe's largest synagogue when it was built in 1671. The architect, Elias Bouman, was inspired by the Temple of Solomon in Jerusalem, although the building's classical lines are fairly typical of Amsterdam.

☎ 624 53 51
✉ Mr Visserplein 3
€ €4.50/3.50 ⏲ 10am-4pm Sun-Fri, services 9am Sat 🚊 9, 14 ♿ good

Spaarndammer Neighbourhood (1, C2)

Behind Westerpark is the wonderful Spaarndammer area, built in the first decades of the 20th century when socialism was in the ascendant. The highlight of the area is the Shipbuilding, taking up a whole block between Zaanstraat and Oostzaanstraat. It was completed in 1920 and features a school and over 100 apartments. The courtyard at Oostzaanstraat 1–21 is a must-see.
✉ Spaarndammerstraat & Zaanstraat 🚊 3, 12, 16, 24

Stopera (2, E7)

Officially called the Stadhuis-Opera, this chunky white city-hall-cum-stage (1986) has been dubbed 'Stopera' for the protests that delayed its construction for nearly two decades. One critic quipped it had 'all the charms of an Ikea chair'.
☎ 625 54 55 🖥 www .hetmuziektheater.nl

✉ Waterlooplein 22
🚊 9, 14 ♿ good

Trippenhuis (2, E6)

Making their fortune in metals, artillery and ammunition, the wealthy Trip brothers had this house built in the 17th century. It's a grey-stone mansion with Corinthian pilasters across two houses, with false middle windows. Back then folks were obviously more open about being in the arms trade: the chimneys are shaped like mortars.
✉ Kloveniersburgwal 29 € free 🚊 4, 9, 16, 24, 25 M Nieuwmarkt ♿ good

Tuschinskitheater (2, C8)

The Tuschinskitheater (built in 1921) blends Art Deco and Amsterdam School architecture, and the interiors (including acres of red carpet and enormous chandeliers) are so ornate as to be almost camp. It must be the loveliest cinema in the entire country. You can peek in the lobby, but to really taste the 1920s style, catch a film in the main auditorium (p88).

☎ 626 26 33 🖥 www .pathe.nl in Dutch
✉ Reguliersbreestraat 26 ⏲ noon-10pm 🚊 4, 9, 14, 24, 25 ♿ excellent

Vondelkerk (3, A2)

One of Amsterdam's prettiest churches, this 19th-century neoclassical gem by Pierre Cuypers is named after poet Joost van den Vondel, the Dutch Shakespeare.
✉ Vondelstraat 77
⏲ 8am-6pm 🚊 1, 6 ♿ good

Zuiderkerk (2, E6)

Amsterdam's first custom-built Protestant church was based on a Catholic design but without the choir. A tile in the entrance recalls that it served as a morgue during WWII. Today it's primarily a planning and public-housing information centre with audiovisual exhibits. Climb the tower from 1 June to 30 September for a great view.
☎ 622 29 62 ✉ Zuiderkerkhof € €3 (for tower) ⏲ noon-5pm Mon-Fri (to 8pm Thu), tower 2-4pm Wed-Sat 🚊 9, 14 M Nieuwmarkt ♿ fair (none for tower)

The unstoppable Stopera, built despite intense local opposition to the design

PARKS & GARDENS

Amsterdam has more trees per square kilometre than any other European city, an aspect often obscured on the ground by the density of its streets and canals. Vondelpark (p18) is the tired urbanite's prime oasis, but there are scores of smaller parks and gardens where you can soak up the rays. In spring, these beautiful places burst with tulips, hyacinths and daffodils.

> ### Ice Skating
> When the park ponds and canals freeze over, the blades come out in force. If you can get hold of a pair of skates, remember to take local advice and be extra careful as people drown under the ice every year. There's a small skating rink at Museumplein (see below), charging around €6 for skates.

Amstelpark (1, D6)
This rambling green space is worth a look for its redolent rose garden. There are pleasant cafés in the grounds, and outside the southern end is a sparkling example of an Amsterdam windmill (the De Rieker, thrown into action only on the second Saturday in May, National Windmill Day, p79). Bicycles aren't allowed in the park.
⊠ Europaboulevard
☼ dawn-dusk 🚌 50, 51
♿ excellent

Amsterdamse Bos (1, B6)
On weekends, world-weary urbanites flock to the Bos (forest), the city's largest park, to enjoy its 940 hectares of lakes and meadows. Laid out in the 1930s, it is almost three times the size of Central Park and 20 times larger than Vondelpark, so it never seems crowded.
☎ 643 14 14
⊠ Koenenkade 56
☼ 24hr 🚌 170, 171, 172; 70 (circuit in forest)
🚊 5 ♿ excellent

Museumplein (3, B3)
A stretch of road that hosted Nazi rallies in the 1940s and 400,000 anti-nuke protestors in 1981, this vast expanse behind the Rijksmuseum was transformed into a park in 1999. It's hard not to be impressed with the sheer size of this, Amsterdam's biggest square.
⊠ Paulus Potterstraat
☼ 24hr 🚊 2, 5 🚌 63, 145, 170, 197 ♿ excellent

Oosterpark (1, E4)
Oosterpark was laid out in the 1880s to accommodate the nouveaux riches of the city's diamond traders, who moved to the area with money to burn. The district's lower-middle-class heritage has since vanished, but this sprawling English-style park just south of the Tropenmuseum is particularly lovely in spring (and lures ice-skaters to its tiny lakes in winter).
⊠ 's-Gravesandestraat
☼ dawn-dusk 🚊 3, 6, 10 ♿ excellent

Vondelark not quite big enough? Visit Amsterdamse Bos

RICHARD NEBESKY

Sarphatipark (3, E4)

This English-style park was named after the energetic 19th-century philanthropist Samuel Sarphati. It's a delightful spot for a picnic lunch, amid the many ponds, fountains and garrulous ducks on the edge of a working-class district.

✉ **Ceintuurbaan**
☽ **dawn-dusk** 🚊 3, 4, 12 ♿ **excellent**

Wertheim Park (4, A5)

Just opposite the Hortus Botanicus gardens is an intimate nook overlooked by most tourists: the canalside Wertheim Park. It contains the Auschwitz Monument designed by Dutch writer Jan Wolkers, a poignant work featuring a split urn, embedded in the ground, that once held the ashes of Jews who died in Buchenwald concentration camp. Despite this grim note, it's a lovely place to sit and daydream in the summer.

✉ **Plantage Parklaan**
☽ **dawn-dusk** 🚊 9, 14 ♿ **excellent**

Westerpark (1, C2)

Just northwest of the Jordaan and well worth a visit, the lovely Westerpark awaits with a tangle of paths, shrubbery and some intriguing public art (check the Floating Headless Lady in the central pond). The adjacent Westergasfabriek cultural centre (p90), drama school and film studios, open 24 hours a day, make for lively company.

✉ **Haarlemmerweg**
☽ **24hr** 🚌 18, 22 ♿ **excellent**

QUIRKY AMSTERDAM

Casa Rosso (2, D5)

Spot the stone penis fountain and you know you've reached Amsterdam's best erotic theatre. It has a slick live-sex show and, unlike other grim palaces of pump, its well-choreographed show is as much about entertainment as heavy breathing. Buck's night revellers tend to go to the Bananen Bar, a nearby sex show beloved of drunken men and banana purveyors (they get through 7kg of them a night).

☎ 627 89 54 🖥 www .casarosso.nl ✉ Oudezijds Achterburgwal 106 € €25 or €40 incl 5 drinks

☽ 8pm-3am 🚊 4, 9, 16, 24, 25 ♿ good

The hard-to-miss fountain outside Casa Rosso

MARTIN MOOS

Condomerie Het Gulden Vlies (2, D4)

So many condoms, so many choices: a good slogan for life, and also that of the Condomerie, which stocks over 100 brands of condom from Durex and Hot Rubber to Benetton. Inch for inch, no-one knows their rubber like these guys.

☎ 627 41 74 🖥 www .condomerie.com ✉ 141 Warmoesstraat € free ☽ 11am-6pm Mon-Sat 🚊 4, 9, 16, 24, 25 ♿ fair

EnergeticA (4, D6)

This electrifying museum devoted to energy techniques

A Likable Lunatic

In the 19th century, Amsterdam's city council regarded doctor, chemist and visionary Samuel Sarphati as an amiable nutter. But look at what this oddball achieved: he established the city's rubbish collection; founded Holland's first bread factory; began an abattoir and trades and business schools; and built the prestigious Amstel InterContinental (p100) and the Palace of People's Industry (which burnt down in 1929, on the site of today's Nederlandse Bank). For each project everyone told him he was crazy — something to remember next time someone tells you the same (unless, of course, they're right).

and household appliances was opened in 2003, in a former power station. Galleries are devoted to the development of everything from toasters and early washing machines to electric lights and TV. There's antique examples of all of them; best of all are the early refrigerators, which are very cool. The section devoted to lifts (elevators) is wonderfully uplifting. A high-voltage place to spend a few hours. ☎ 422 12 27 ⌨ www .energetica.nl in Dutch ✉ Hoogte Kadijk 400 € €3 🕙 10am-4pm Mon-Fri 🚊 9, 14 🚌 22, 32 ♿ excellent

Hash Marihuana Hemp Museum (2, D5)

The place to come for all the dope on dope. It's pokey and somewhat dishevelled, but this museum still boasts a kaleidoscope of displays that go all the way back to the roots of marijuana use (first recorded in China in 3727 BC). However, it could prove dull for those not completely in the thrall of the wonderful weed, with some exhibits so biased they read like propaganda for marijuana's role in the path to true enlightenment. ☎ 623 59 61 ✉ Oudezijds Achterburgwal 148 € €5.70 🕙 11am-10pm 🚊 4, 9, 16, 24, 25 ♿ good

Kattenkabinet (3, D1)

Amsterdam has a pussy obsession. Find out how deep it runs with a visit to the Kattenkabinet, which claims to be the world's only museum devoted to cats.

The admission fee preys upon feline fans, who tend to be obsessive sorts, but it's probably worth it to see the (real live) moggies that guard the works. ☎ 626 53 78 ⌨ www .kattenkabinet.nl ✉ Herengracht 497 € €4.50 🕙 10am-2pm Mon-Fri, 1-5pm Sat & Sun 🚊 1, 2, 5, 16, 24, 25 ♿ fair

Max Euwe Centrum (3, B2)

Max Euwe was the chess world champion from 1935 to 1937, and the Dutch love him. At this chess centre, you'll find more than 11,000 publications on chess, a huge video archive and scores of chess computers at which you can practise for free. If you fancy a game with a human, ask for the list of chess pubs where you can walk in and ask anyone for a friendly game. ☎ 625 70 17 ⌨ www .maxeuwe.nl ✉ Max Euweplein 30a € free 🕙 10.30am-4pm Tue-Fri & first Sat each month 🚊 1, 2, 5, 6, 7, 10 ♿ poor

Poezenboot (2, C2)

Homeless cats find a whole lotta lovin' at this houseboat on the Singel, where around 60 strays get the care and attention they've missed out on elsewhere. The *Poezenboot* (cat boat) survives on donations and the love of the volunteers who work there. Pay a visit and buy a postcard while you coo over a tomcat. ☎ 625 87 94 ⌨ www .poezenboot.nl ✉ near Singel 40 € free 🕙 1-3pm 🚊 1, 2, 5, 13, 17 ♿ fair

Watch the sparks fly at EnergeticA

RICHARD NEBESKY

AMSTERDAM FOR CHILDREN

Amsterdammers take a relaxed view of children, at tourist attractions and in pubs and restaurants. Many special events geared towards kids take place throughout the year. Check the monthly *Uitkrant* listings magazine under 'Agenda Jeugd'; otherwise contact the **Amsterdam Uit Buro** (5, C6; ☎ 0900-91 91 100, per min €0.40; Leidseplein 26) for special children's events.

Aviodrome Schiphol (6, E3)
This national aviation museum is a hit with all shoe sizes. Sit in the cockpit of old planes such as the Wright Brothers' historic flyer and a triplane used by Baron von Richthofen (aka the Red Baron). A section is devoted to space flight.
☎ 406 80 00 🖳 www .aviodrome.nl ✉ Schiphol Centre, Westelijke Randweg 201 € €6/4.50 🕑 10am-5pm (closed Mon, noon-5pm Sat & Sun Oct-Apr) 🚆 Schiphol Airport ♿ excellent

Circustheater Elleboog (5, B5)
Parents will be proud: children aged four to 17 can learn circus skills including juggling and clowning, and then perform them for their parents and friends at the end of the day. Phone ahead for exact prices and times.
☎ 626 93 70 🖳 www .elleboog.nl ✉ Passeer-dersgracht 32 € €6-15 🕑 varies 🚊 7, 10 ♿ good

Madame Tussaud's Scenerama (2, C5)
Tussaud's spent €4 million on a refurbishment in 2003, but it's done little to improve the grim nature of this grotesquely expensive wax museum. Of course, that doesn't stop the lines being a mile long on weekends and might not stop your little ones demanding their hit of wax global superstars.
☎ 622 92 39 🖳 www .madame-tussauds.com ✉ Dam 20 (by Peek & Cloppenburg) € adult/ child 5-16/under 5 €19/€10/free 🕑 10am-5.30pm 🚊 4, 9, 16, 24, 25 ♿ excellent

Baby-sitting
Baby-sitters charge from €5 per hour, and there's often an additional €4 to €5 for weekend nights. Agencies tend to use university students (female and male). Try **Oppascentrale Kriterion** (☎ 624 58 48; Roetersstraat 170; 🕑 9-11am & 4.30-8pm), the best known in town, or **Oppascentrale De Peuterette** (☎ 679 67 93; 🕑 3-4pm Tue-Thu). Some upmarket hotels also offer baby-sitting (see listings in the Sleeping chapter, p99).

Missing your moggie back home? Try this one for size at Kattenkabinet (p37)

Mirandabad (1, D5)

Get some aquatic action at this complex with a wave machine, beach, whirlpool and elaborate, tunnelled slides. There are indoor and outdoor pools – enough to fill a day out with the tots. ☎ 64280 80 ⌂ De Miran-dalaan 9 € €4.50/3.50 🕐 7am-10pm 🚊 4 ♿ good

Tropenmuseum Junior (1, E4)

The Tropenmuseum boasts a special section for six- to 12-year-olds, which is mostly in Dutch but also offers English-language programs from June to September (call ahead to check times). Their exalted aim is to promote intercultural understanding, a UN-like goal livened up with great hands-on exhibits. (The admission fee is in addition to the Tropenmuseum admission; see p22.) ☎ 568 82 33 💻 www .kindermuseum.nl ✉ Linnaeusstraat 2 € €1.60 🕐 1-6pm Wed, 11am-6pm Sat & Sun 🚊 3, 6, 10 ♿ excellent

Other Kiddie Favourites

- Artis Zoo (p20)
- Canal cruises (p48)
- NEMO (p27)
- Vondelpark (p18)
- Zaanse Schans (p44)
- Egyptian models at the Allard Pierson Museum (p26)

Strictly for pros: the challenging sport of soda-bottle fishing at the Vondelpark

Tun Fun (2, F7)

For 11 years, a vast, 4000-sq-metre traffic underpass below Mr Visserplein sat unused, before it got a very creative and very Dutch treatment: in 2003, it was turned into a deeply fun indoor playground. Kids aged one to 12 can build, climb, roll, draw, play indoor soccer and dance. There's a restaurant and café for the parents to play in. Note that kids can visit Tun Fun only if accompanied by an adult. It gets unbelievably crowded (and loud!) when the weather's bad. ☎ 689 43 00 💻 www .tunfun.nl ✉ Mr Visser-plein 7 € adult/child 1-12 free/€7 🕐 10am-7pm 🚊 9, 14 ♿ good

Travel to the tropics and beyond at the Tropenmuseum Junior

Out & About

WALKING TOURS
Walking the Canals

Start at Queen Beatrix's residence on Dam Square, the **Koninklijk Paleis** (**1**; p19), flanked by the impressive **Nieuwe Kerk** (**2**; p33). Cross the broad Nieuwezijds Voorburgwal towards the Singel, the heart of the old merchants' district. Atop the Torensteeg Bridge stands the clay-like statue of **Multatuli** (**3**), pen name of the author Eduard Dowes Dekker.

Continue north to Herenmarkt, with its 17th-century **West Indisch Huis** (**4**), and turn west down Brouwersgracht. Walking south on Prinsengracht you'll see the imposing **Noorderkerk** (**5**). Make a dogleg into Keizersgracht, with the curious **House with the Heads** (**6**; p32) opposite. At peaceful Leliegracht, by the **Greenpeace Building** (**7**; p32), return to Prinsengracht to pass the **Anne Frankhuis** (**8**; p10) and the soaring tower of the **Westerkerk** (**9**; p23) beyond. Further south stop at **Van Puffelen** (**10**; p84), a typical brown café at No 377.

On Keizersgracht you can't miss the quirky **Felix Meritis building** (**11**; p91), home to a one-time Enlightenment society, then alternative theatre and now cultural centre. Pass the **Bijbels Museum** (**12**; p26) on Herengracht into the **Spui** (**13**). The gate on the northern side into the **Begijnhof** (**14**; p21) is sometimes open; otherwise you'll have to go round to the side entrance. The **Amsterdams Historisch Museum** (**15**; p16) is just up the street. Continue north to **Magna Plaza** (**16**; p50), a stunning former post office that's been turned into a shopping mall.

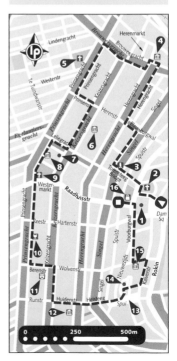

distance 3.9km duration 3hr
▶ start Dam Square
● end Magna Plaza

Prime place for a stroll: Prinsengracht, in the Jordaan neighbourhood

Art & Nature Walk

Art attack: Van Gogh Museum (foreground), Rijksmuseum (background), Museumplein

What better place to start than at the **Rijksmuseum** (**1**; p8)? Walk through its beautiful underpass to Museumplein, a monumental grassy expanse for lolling, walking and open-air concerts. The **Van Gogh Museum** (**2**; p9) and its modern, mussel-like annexe are on the southwestern edge next to the contemporary **Stedelijk Museum** (**3**; p15), which is closed until at least 2006. For picnic goodies, there's a big Albert Heijn supermarket here, too. The neoclassical **Concertgebouw** (**4**; p92) is in plain view across Van Baerlestraat.

Weave northwest through a quiet residential quarter to **Vondelpark** (**5**; p18); highlights in the park include the **petting zoo** (**6**), a **rose garden** (**7**) and an **open-air theatre** (**8**). Refreshment options abound: enjoy coffee and cake in the **Round Blue Teahouse** (**9**) or the parkside **Vertigo** (**10**; ☎ 612 31 21) at the **Nederlands Filmmuseum** (p88). Admire the **Vondelkerk** (**11**), a pretty 19th-century church turned office complex, before either heading back into the leafy oasis of the park to while away the afternoon or striking out along Vondelstraat towards the buzz of Leidseplein. Take tram No 1 back towards the central canal belt.

distance 4km **duration** 4hr
▶ **start** Rijksmuseum
⦿ **end** Leidseplein

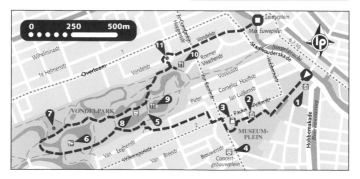

Red-Light Ramble

Begin at the **Nationaal Monument** (**1**) and head north along Damrak past the present-day stock exchange to the elegant **Beurs van Berlage** (**2**; p30), the old Bourse. Dip into the red-light district en route to the venerable **Oude Kerk** (**3**; p13). Just north of here is the **Museum Amstelkring** (**4**; p27). A jump over the Oudezijds Voorburgwal takes you past the **Casa Rosso** (**5**; p36), the famous erotic theatre in the heart of the red-light district (also known as the Walletjes).

From here you'll reach Nieuwmarkt, with its multitowered **De Waag** (**6**; Weigh House, p31). Stop at De Waag for a great lunch or snack if you're in the mood; it's now a wonderful restaurant open for lunch and dinner. The impossibly narrow **Trippenhuis** (**7**; p34), once owned by armaments dealers, is just south of here. Wander on to the elegant **Zuiderkerk** (**8**; p34), with the 17th-century **Pintohuis** (**9**) opposite. Now home to a library, it was restored by Isaac de Pinto, the Jewish refugee who founded the VOC (see p33). **Rembrandthuis** (**10**; p28) is a few doors down.

A leisurely sweep down Jodenbreestraat will take you past the **Mozes en Aaronkerk** (**11**), formerly a clandestine Catholic church where Franz Liszt played his best-ever concert. Fifty metres to the southeast is the **Joods Historisch Museum** (**12**; p26). Surrounding the **Stopera** (**13**; p34), Amsterdam's opera house and city hall, is the Waterlooplein **flea market** (**14**; p51; ⏰9am-5pm Mon-Fri, 8.30am-5.30pm Sat). Have a look around the bustling market before crossing the **Blauwbrug** (**15**; Blue Bridge).

Near Rembrandtplein, stop at the charming **Museum Willet-Holthuysen** (**16**; p27). Cross the River Amstel to the **Allard Pierson Museum** (**17**; p26) for some archaeology then head back to Dam Square via the colourful hotel-lined lane, Nes. Back at the square, take a peek into the lobby of the **Grand Hotel Krasnapolsky** (**18**, p100).

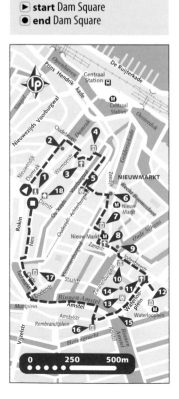

distance 4km **duration** 3hr
▶ **start** Dam Square
● **end** Dam Square

Eastern Islands Walk

The Eastern harbour, with its 8000 new homes, is Amsterdam's show-case of modern residential architecture. Catch bus No 32 or 39 to the Piet Heinkade and Kattenburgerstraat intersection. Walk under the old warehouse to the **Jan Schaefer Bridge** (**1**), named after a 1980s social-housing activist (motto: 'You can't live in claptrap'). Turn east (right) onto Sumatrakade, on Java Eiland's north, and walk eastwards; on your right note the **canals** (**2**) and the unique bridges. Within the apartment blocks, look at some of the gardens, themed (from west to east) winter, autumn, summer and spring.

Continue to KNSM Eiland (named after the Royal Netherlands Steamship Company, which was once based here). Carry on west towards the Verbindingsdam (Con-necting Dam) and cross to Sporen-burg. Turn right onto Veemkade and stop for a drink at **Odessa** (**3**; p85) . Behind the shopping centre you'll see the tower of the **Lloyd Hotel** (**4**; p100), a former prison now resurrected as a hip hotel.

Return to Sporenburg and walk around the cutting-edge **Whale Building** (**5**), with its eye-catching slanted roofline and zinc scales. Peer through the gate at its inacces-sible garden, a landscaping work of art. Continue to Sporenburg's tip and walk across the bright-red **Dinosaur Bridge** (**6**) to Borneo Ei-land and back.

Keeping fit on KNSM Eiland

distance 3.5km **duration** 2hr
▶ **start** Jan Schaefer Bridge
● **end** Sporenburg

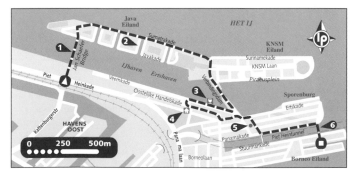

DAY TRIPS
Utrecht (6, F3)

Historic Utrecht was the ecclesiastical centre of the Low Countries from the early Middle Ages. Today it's an antique shell surrounding an increasingly modern interior, lorded over by the tower of the Dom (Cathedral), the Netherlands' tallest church tower at 112m. The 14th-century canals, once-bustling wharves and cellars now brim with chic shops, restaurants and cafés.

INFORMATION
25km southeast of Amsterdam
- 🚊 1hr from Amsterdam Centraal
- 💻 www.utrecht.nl
- € €8 return by train
- ℹ️ VVV (☎ 0900-128 87 32; Vinkenburgstraat 19; per min €0.40); Centraal Museum (☎ 030-236 23 63; Nicolaaskerkhof 10; 🕑 Tue-Sun 11am-5pm; €8/4)
- 🍴 De Winkel van Sinkel (☎ 030-251 06 93; Oudegracht 158)

The large student population (Utrecht is home to the country's largest university) adds spice to a once largely church-oriented community. Locals proudly claim that bars and cafés stay open far later than in Amsterdam, to cater to student needs. It's a simple task to drink all night at one of these bars and still make it back to Amsterdam before sunrise by train.

The Centraal Museum has one of Holland's best collections of Golden Age paintings, and the world's largest collection of work by architect and furniture designer Gerrit Rietveld (1888–1964), one of the De Stijl artists.

Zaanse Schans (6, E2)

This museum-piece village on the Zaan River is admittedly kitschy but has its merits: authentic windmills, some intriguing workshops and historic exhibits. The village was one of the world's first light industrial regions, with over 700 windmills powering flour and paint production. Houses have been carted in from around the country to re-create the 17th-century community. On a sunny day it can be fun despite the crowds. Several attractions are free, such as the Albert Hein colonial goods shop, a cheesemaker's shop and a clog factory.

In neighbouring **Zaandam** (6, F2), pay a quick visit to the small wooden cabin at Krimp 23, where Peter the Great of Russia lived incognito for five months in 1697, working as a shipwright's apprentice on the wharves nearby so he could help improve the Russian navy.

INFORMATION
16km northwest of Amsterdam
- 🚊 30min Amsterdam Centraal to Koog Zaandijk, then an 8min signposted walk to Kalverringdijk
- 💻 www.zaanseschans.nl
- € per exhibit €3-6, Tsar Peterhuisje €2/1.50
- 🕑 exhibits 10am-5pm Tue-Sun Mar-Oct, to 5pm Sat & Sun Nov-Feb; Tsar Peterhuisje 10am-1pm & 2-5pm Tue-Fri, 1-5pm Sat
- ℹ️ VVV (☎ 075-616 22 21 or 635 17 47; Gedempte Gracht 76, Zandaam)

Wet and windy: perfect windmill weather

Haarlem (6, E2)

Parts of this vibrant city, with its picturesque bridges and winding alleys, rival anything Amsterdam has to offer. It has a couple of great museums that can easily be covered in a day if you don't also plan to visit the world's largest flower gardens at **Keukenhof** (6, E3), in nearby Lisse.

Haarlem Centraal train station is an Art Deco masterpiece and probably the most beautiful station in the country. You can sense the locals are well off: check out some of the fancier boutiques and antique shops along Kruisstraat on the walk into town. Like Amsterdam, Haarlem also has many *hofjes* (courtyards), although these aren't closed to the public, unlike so many of Amsterdam's.

The impressive late-Gothic Grote Kerk (aka Sint Bavokerk), on Grote Markt, is home to a stunning Müller organ. One of the most magnificent in the world, it was once played by a 10-year-old Mozart.

A must-see for fans of Dutch painting is the Frans Hals Museum,

INFORMATION
15km west of Amsterdam
- 🚆 15min from Amsterdam Centraal
- 🖥 www.haarlem.nl
- ℹ️ VVV (☎ 0900-61 61 600, Stationsplein 1; per min €0.40); Frans Hals Museum (☎ 023-511 57 75; Groot Heiligland 62; 🕙 11am-5pm Mon-Sat, 1-5pm Sun; €5); Keukenhof (☎ 025-246 55 55; Stationsweg 166a, Lisse; 🕙 8am-7.30pm late Mar-late May; €8/4.50); Teylers Museum (☎ 023-531 90 10; Spaarne 16; 🕙 10am-5pm Tue-Sat, noon-5pm Sun; €5.50/1.50); Grote Kerk (Grote Markt; 10am-4pm Mon-Sat)
- 🍴 De Componist (☎ 023-532 88 53; Korte Veerstraat 1)

10 minutes' walk south of Grote Markt, which features many of the master's group portraits as well as works by other greats, including Jacob van Ruysdael and Pieter Bruegel the Younger. The museum is in an almshouse where the painter spent his final impoverished years. Teylers Museum, the oldest museum in the country (1778), has an odd but noteworthy collection including drawings by Michelangelo and Raphael.

Listen up: Grote Kerk is famous for its Müller organ, once played by a precocious Mozart in 1766

Leiden (6, E3)

This cheerful city has an intellectual aura generated by 20,000 students, and is home to the country's oldest university (founded in 1575). The institution was a present from William the Silent (William of Orange), a reward for withstanding a long Spanish siege in 1574. One-third of the residents starved before the Spaniards retreated on 3 October, a date still celebrated as the annual town festival. Most sights lie within a confusing web of central canals, about a 10-minute walk southeast of the train station.

Many Dutch come to Leiden for the town's 11 museums. The Rijksmuseum van Oudheden (National Museum of Antiquities) has a world-class display of Greek, Roman and Egyptian finds. Pride of place is the Temple of Taffeh, a gift of then Egyptian president Anwar Sadat to the Netherlands for helping to save ancient monuments from flood. With a focus on the former Dutch colonies, the Rijksmuseum voor Volkenkunde (National Ethnology Museum) has even better Indonesian displays than those found at Amsterdam's Tropenmuseum (p22). De Valk (the Falcon), a museum in Leiden's landmark windmill, blows away notions that these contraptions were a Dutch invention.

The Hortus Botanicus, Europe's oldest botanical garden (1587), is a real treat. Sited in a velvety rear plot near a large canal, it has well-tended beds and explosions of tropical colour. Check out the enormous lily pads in the top floor of the steamy hothouse.

INFORMATION

23km southwest of Amsterdam

🚆 every 15min from Amsterdam Centraal

🖥 www.leiden.nl

ℹ VVV (☎ 0900-61 61 600; per min €0.40; Stationsplein 210); Hortus Botanicus (☎ 071-527 72 49; Rapenburg 73, 🕙 10am-5pm, closed Sat Oct-Feb; €4/2); Rijksmuseum van Oudheden (☎ 071-516 31 63; Rapenburg 28; 🕙 10am-5pm Tue-Sun, €4/2.50); Rijksmuseum voor Volkenkunde (☎ 071-516 88 00; Steenstraat 1; 🕙 10am-5pm Tue-Fri, noon-5pm Sat & Sun; €4.50/3); De Valk (☎ 071-516 53 53; Tweede Binnenvestgracht 1; 🕙 10am-5pm Tue-Sat, 1-5pm Sun, €4/3)

Lively times in Leiden, world renowned for its university and sociable student scene

ORGANISED TOURS

There's a tour to suit every taste in Amsterdam, ranging from cycling and walking to boat and bus tours. Avoid boat tours on rainy days, because it can get claustrophobic when those windows steam up.

City Tours

GVB (2, E2)

If you're feeling nostalgic, jump on the 1920s tourist tram – leaving from opposite Victoria Hotel (2, D3) in front of Centraal Station – and trundle past the main sights. The GVB also has a candlelight and dinner tram. Inquire at their office in front of Centraal Station.
☎ 460 53 53 ☐ www .gvb.nl ✉ Damrak 1-5 € €8/6 ⌚ half-hourly Sun & holidays Jun-Sep

Keytours (2, D3)

In summer, Keytours runs four-hour city tours (2.30pm daily) by bus. The route includes the Rijksmuseum and a diamond factory. The one-hour canal cruises, leaving every 30 minutes, are better value at €8.
☎ 623 50 51 ☐ www .keytours.nl ✉ Damrak 19 € €8-22

Lindbergh Tours (2, D3)

City sightseeing bus tours with commentary (€10, 2½ hours) leave daily at 10am and 2.30pm in summer (10am only in winter). Lindbergh also does a red-light district walking tour from 8pm to 10pm each night in summer.
☎ 622 27 66 ☐ www .lindbergh.nl ✉ Damrak 26 € €6-19.50

Red-Light District Tour (2, E2)

Under the auspices of the VVV, this tour lasts about two hours. Knowledgeable guides cheerfully cover all you need to know about prostitution and drug use in Amsterdam.
☎ 624 57 20 ☐ www .robvanhulst.nl ✉ VVV office (in front of Centraal Station) or at Zeedijk 34 € €15 ⌚ 6pm Fri & Sat nights

Urban Home & Garden Tours

These well-regarded tours look at Amsterdam dwellings from the perspective of home, garden and even gable. Visits include 18th-century, 19th-century and contemporary homes.
☎ 688 12 43 ☐ www .uhgt.nl ✉ Herengracht 605 € €37.50 (incl lunch)

Bicycle Tours

Cycletours Holland (2, A4)

This company offers a variety of tours of Holland by bicycle and barge boat sleeping 15 to 30 people. A one-week tour (departing Saturday) in a two-berth cabin with private amenities costs €740; the five-day tour costs €330. Write ahead for a brochure and reservations.
☎ 627 40 98 ☐ www .cycletours.com ✉ Keizersgracht 181 € varies ⌚ summer only

Let's Go (2, E2)

Join a very professional tour (6½ hours; €24.50 not including train tickets) to villages, castles and windmills east of Amsterdam. Departure is from the VVV office in front of Centraal Station – you take the train and mount your bike at the other end. They also do an excellent historical tour (€9) around the old city.
☎ 600 18 09 ☐ www .letsgo-amsterdam.com ✉ VVV office, Centraal Station € €9-24.50

The Dutch conveyance of choice (Dam Square)

RICHARD NEBESKY

Mike's Bike Tours (3, C2)
Mike's four-hour tours take you both around the centre of town and into the countryside, where you can see windmills, cheese farms and the like. Guides really know their city, and there's a high probability you'll end the tour at a pub.
☎ 622 79 70 🖳 www .mikesbikeamsterdam .com ✉ Meet at entrance B of the Rijksmuseum, Stadhouderskade 42 € €22 ⌚ Mar-Nov

Yellow Bike Guided Tours (2, C3)
Amsterdam's largest bike-tour operator offers three-hour tours around town and all-day tours (6½ hours) to the sleepy village of Broek in Waterland, 15km north of Amsterdam.
☎ 620 69 40 🖳 www .yellowbike.nl ✉ Nieuwezijds Kolk 29 € €17-25 ⌚ summer only

Boat Tours
GVB (2, E2)
GVB leads a ferry circuit of city-centre sights, starting near Centraal Station and heading up the IJ River past the Eastern Islands.

They also organise hydrofoil and catamaran trips to other destinations. You can buy tickets from the GVB office in front of Centraal Station.
☎ 460 53 53 🖳 www .gvb.nl ✉ Pier 8 De Ruijterkade € €7/5 ⌚ noon, 2pm & 4pm

Lovers (2, D2)
Choose from a hop-on-hop-off canal ferry (€19.50 per day), a one-hour canal cruise (€8.50), or the very popular candlelight cruise (€27, book ahead).
☎ 530 10 90 🖳 www .lovers.nl in Dutch ✉ Pier 7 De Ruijterkade € €8.50-€27

St Nicolaas Boat Club (3, B1)
The Boom Chicago comedy troupe (see p91) helps organise tours, run by a nonprofit boating organisation, on charismatic old chug boats. The 90-minute trip trundles the canals of the red-light district. You're welcome to toke on a joint on board (hell, it's positively encouraged). Head to boom-Bar on Leidseplein to book.

A building with a classical bent – Koninklijk Paleis

☎ 423 01 01 (bookings in person only) 🖳 www .boomchicago.nl ✉ Leidseplein 12 € by donation ⌚ noon-midnight Apr-Oct (depending on numbers)

Gay-Themed Tours
Gay History Walking Tour (5, C2)
This two-hour tour traces the history of two 18th-century Amsterdammers sentenced to death for being gay. It includes entry to the Koninklijk Paleis (if open), the site of the executions.
☎ 672 39 93 🖳 www .fantasycity.org ✉ meet at Pink Point, Westerkerk € €18 ⌚ May-Aug

The Really Queer Grand Tour (2, D4)
A four-hour tour covering the red-light district, gay leather area, bars, coffeeshops, secret alleys and lots more. This tour includes a Canal Bus pass (value €15) that's valid until noon the next day.
☎ 672 39 93 🖳 www .fantasycity.org ✉ Warmoesstraat 60 € €38

No, it's not the alcohol. It's the slanted De Sluyswacht (p85), here since 1695.

Shopping

For centuries, goods available nowhere else in Europe were found in Amsterdam. The Dutch were experts at plundering the tastiest morsels from their many colonies, such as spices from the Spice Islands (now Indonesia) and coffee from Ethiopia. Though the sun has long since set on the Dutch empire, Amsterdam remains the place to seek out the unusual, quirky and original.

Set against a backdrop of scenic canals, gabled canal houses and cobblestone streets are clusters of gorgeous boutiques, hip art galleries and one-off speciality stores. Renowned for its diamonds, flowers and delftware, Amsterdam's real strengths are its fashion and homeware stores. But if sex, drugs 'n' *rokerij* (coffeeshops) are on your agenda, you'll find the greatest abundance of sex paraphernalia, magic mind-alterers and dope emporiums at your disposal.

Riffling through records at the Noordermarkt (p51), Jordaan

All the major retail precincts are within the canals, or not far outside, so getting around on foot is easy. And the amiability of Dutch salespeople, with their perfect English, makes shopping a breeze. Ironically, for a city with such a rich trading history, very little bargaining goes on: it's discouraged in all stores and most markets. Major credit cards are accepted at department stores and boutiques, but many small shops are unequipped or unwilling to take plastic.

All *winkels* (shops) open Monday to Saturday, and most larger stores open Sunday. Normal shopping hours are noon to 6pm Monday, 10am to 6pm Tuesday, Wednesday, Friday and Saturday and 10am to 9pm Thursday. Shops trading on Sundays generally open from noon to 5pm.

Hot Shop Spots

Amsterdam's main shopping areas are:

- Western Canal Belt (2, A5) Quirky speciality shops and fashion boutiques with designer shoes, upmarket and vintage clothing; gifts, tourist tack and books on crowded Leidsestraat.
- Jordaan (Map 5) Small, offbeat boutiques and galleries; vintage clothing stores, specialist homeware shops and second-hand record stores.
- Kalverstraat (2, B5) & Nieuwendijk (2, C4) Mainstream consumer paradise: department stores, fashion-chain emporiums (especially for teenagers) and too many mobile-phone stores to count.
- PC Hooftstraat (3, B3) All the big designer names: Donna Karan, Armani, Bally et al, plus a sprinkling of lifestyle and jewellery shops and chi-chi perfumeries.
- Spiegelkwartier (3, C2) This area is a browser's mecca of commercial art galleries and antique shops selling everything from 17th-century delftware to Buddhist prayer bowls.

DEPARTMENT STORES

Bijenkorf (2, C5)
Five floors of perfect stock and three cafés make this the city's favourite department store. The usual brands are here (DKNY, Polo, Ralph Lauren) as are funkier labels G-Star and W&LT. Lit up at night, the building looks spectacular.
☎ 621 80 80 ✉ Dam 1 ☽ 11am-7pm Mon, 9.30am-7pm Tue & Wed, to 9pm Thu & Fri, to 6pm Sat, noon-6pm Sun ⛟ 4, 9, 16, 24, 25

Hema (2, C4)
Hema is Holland's equivalent of Kmart, but a quick browse will reveal how stylish the Dutch are – if only no-frills shopping was always this hip. Stock up on cute kids' clothes, fab stationery, good-value wines and deli goods, then try the mod cafeteria.
☎ 623 41 76 ✉ Nieuwendijk 174 ☽ 9.30am-6.30pm Mon-Fri (to 9pm Thu), to 6pm Sat, noon-6pm Sun ⛟ 1, 2, 4, 5, 9, 13, 16, 17, 24, 25

Kalvertoren (2, B8)
You'll find the usual brandscape here – Levis, Timberland, Guess etc – and hordes of cashed-up teens spending Daddy's money.
☎ 623 2243 ✉ Singel 457 ☽ 11am-7pm Mon, 10am-7pm Tue, Wed, Fri, to 9pm Thu, to 6pm Sat, noon-6pm Sun ⛟ 1, 2, 4, 5, 9, 13, 16, 17, 24, 25

Magna Plaza (2, B4)
This gorgeous19th-century building (p33) is almost too grand to be a shopping centre. Once the city's main post office, Magna Plaza now hosts over 40 upmarket fashion, gift and jewellery stores. Top shops are America Today (vintage and new Levis), Ordning & Reda (smart stationery) and delightful kids' stores such as Pinokkio (p58).
☎ 626 91 99 ✉ Nieuwezijds Voorburgwal 182 ☽ 11am-7pm Mon, 10am-7pm Tue-Sat (to 9pm Thu), noon-7pm Sun ⛟ 1, 2, 5, 13, 17

Maison de Bonneterie (2, C7)
Exclusive clothes deserve a beautiful setting, and there's none grander than the Maison de Bonneterie. This century-old, family-run store is supplier of clothes to no less than Queen Beatrix.
☎ 531 34 00 ✉ Rokin 140 ☽ noon-6pm Sun-Mon, 10am-6pm Tue-Sat (to 9pm Thu) ⛟ 1, 2, 4, 5, 9, 13, 16, 17, 24, 25

Metz & Co (2, A8)
Like its customers, Metz & Co is a picture of under-stated glamour. Quirky collections by Alexander McQueen and Helmut Lang sit comfortably with tradi-tional labels such as John Smedley and Max Mara. The luxury furnishings and homewares are a dream, as is the top-floor café with city views.
☎ 520 70 36 ✉ Keizers-gracht 455 ☽ 11am-6pm Mon, 9.30am-6pm Tue-Sat (to 9pm Thu), noon-5pm Sun ⛟ 1, 2, 5

Vroom & Dreesmann (2, C7)
It may not be stylish or glam but it's always packed with shoppers picking up quality clothes and home-wares at reasonable prices. Round off with a visit to the extraordinary in-house eatery, La Place.
☎ 622 01 71 ✉ Kalverstraat 201 ☽ 10am-7pm Mon-Fri, to 9pm Sat, noon-6pm Sun ⛟ 1, 2, 4, 5, 9, 13, 16, 17, 24, 25

Megamagnet for upmarket shoppers, Magna Plaza

MARTIN MOOS

MARKETS

Albert Cuypmarkt (3, D4)
Pick up that long-yearned-for pair of fake G-Star jeans at Amsterdam's largest, best-known general market. You'll find fruit and veg, seafood, hardware and homeware stalls among the 350 traders. Don't expect charm or character (and some prices are distinctly touristy), but it's great for watching locals go about their business.
⊠ **Albert Cuypstraat**
☽ 10am-5pm Mon-Sat
🚋 16, 24 , 25

Bloemenmarkt (2, B8)
Thousands of plants, herbs, bulbs and colourful flowers are sold from 15 'floating' stalls permanently moored along the Singel. The market started in the 1860s when gardeners sailed up the Amstel to sell flowers and plants directly from their boats.
⊠ **Singel btwn Koningsplein & Muntplein**
☽ 9.30am-5pm Mon-Sat
🚋 1, 2, 4, 5, 9, 14, 16, 24, 25

Dappermarkt (1, E4)
A locals' market, and the sort of place the Albert Cuypmarkt was before tourists got wind of it. Pick up bargain fish, nuts, fruit, underwear and fake jeans. Dappermarkt is the best place for watching real Amsterdam do its thing.
⊠ **Dapperstraat**
☽ 10am-5pm Mon-Sat
🚋 3, 6, 10, 14

De Looier (5, B5)
Seek out everything from vintage delftware to pre-loved teddy bears at this indoor complex with over 200 antique stalls. Most interesting are the specialist stalls: look for nooks squished full of antique clocks or Bakelite jewellery. On Wednesdays and weekends individual dealers run a flea market.
☎ 624 90 38 ⊠ **Elandsgracht 109** ☽ 11am-5pm Mon-Thu, Sat & Sun
🚋 7, 10

Noordermarkt (2, A2)
Shopping trends come and go, but Amsterdam's neighbourhood markets carry on for centuries. Locals have been legging it to the Noordermarkt since 1627. Mondays sees books, records, vintage clothes and factory seconds being traded. On Saturdays, it has organic food and home-grown produce.
⊠ **Noorderkerkstraat**
☽ 9am-1pm Mon, 10am-3pm Sat 🚋 3, 10

Oudemanhuis Book Market (2, D7)
In operation since the 19th century, this charming market focuses on books, posters, postcards and sheet music. Join students and staff from the nearby University of Amsterdam as they browse hundreds of well-thumbed tomes.
⊠ **Oudemanhuispoort**
☽ 11am-4pm Mon-Fri
🚋 4, 9, 16, 24, 25

Waterlooplein (2, E7)
You need a '70s-style leather jacket, Beastie Boys record and Indian hash pipe, and you need 'em now! Sure, there's junk galore at Amsterdam's most famous flea market, but it's fun sifting through it to find the perfect vintage jacket or handbag. Unlike at other markets, haggling is encouraged.
⊠ **Waterlooplein**
☽ 9am-5pm Mon-Sat
🚋 9, 14 Ⓜ Waterlooplein

Westermarkt (5, C3)
A general goods market that's extremely popular with Jordaan locals for their fruit and veg shopping.
⊠ **Westermarkt**
☽ 9am-1pm Mon
🚋 13, 14, 17

Bringing Bulbs Back Home

Traders at the Bloemenmarkt should be able to tell you if the bulbs you want can be taken home. The Irish Republic and the UK allow an unlimited amount of bulbs to be brought in, as do Canada and the USA (but for the latter two countries you need a certificate for them). Japan permits up to 100 certified bulbs to be imported, while Australia and New Zealand ban their importation altogether.

RICHARD NEBESKY

CLOTHING

Flamboyant boutiques and big-name *haute couture* emporiums are few and far between, though PC Hooftstraat (p49), is the exception that proves the rule. Instead, Amsterdam's streets are lined with one-step-ahead shops stocking stylish, low-key and reasonably priced articles.

DESIGNER GEAR
π (2, D6)

Hipster boys with a deeply couture bent will appreciate the carefully selected range of slick street wear here, ranging from conservatively stylish Helmut Lang numbers to far more out-there fashion of the high-camp variety. ☎ 421 63 29 ✉ Oude Hoogstraat 10 ☽ 10am-6pm Mon-Sat (to 9pm Thu), 1-6pm Sun 🚊 4, 9, 16, 24, 25

Analik (5, C3)

Amsterdam's pre-eminent designer creates feminine pieces for Amsterdam's hippest girls. Have your credit card ready when you enter this graceful boutique – it's difficult to resist the simple, beautiful designs fashioned from top-quality natural textiles.

☎ 422 05 61 ✉ Hartenstraat 36 ☽ 1-6pm Mon, 11am-6pm Tue-Sat (to 9pm Thu) 🚊 1, 2, 5, 13, 14, 17

Cora Kemperman (2, A8)

Cora Kemperman makes comfortable, layered separates and dresses in luxurious natural fabrics such as raw silk, cotton and wool. The easy-to-wear, elegant clothes have quickly made Kemperman one of Holland's favourite designers. ☎ 625 12 84 ✉ Leidsestraat 72 ☽ 10am-6pm Tue-Sat (to 9pm Thu, 7pm Sat), noon-6pm Sun & Mon 🚊 1, 2, 5

Seventyfive (2, E6)

Worship at this temple to trainers with brands such as Royal Elastics, Gola, W&LT, Rizzo and, of course, Nike and Adidas. Prices are more reasonable than in the UK, though true trainer aficionados won't be impressed with the range. Also at Van Woustraat 14 and Haarlemmerdijk 55. ☎ 626 46 11 ✉ Nieuwe Hoogstraat 24 ☽ 10am-6pm 🚊 4, 9, 16, 24, 25 Ⓜ Nieuwmarkt

Shoebaloo (2, A8)

Amsterdam's most sought-after shoes are found at Shoebaloo: drool over imports from Patrick Cox, Miu Miu and Prada Sport, then purchase the less pricey but almost indistinguishable house label. Women's shoes are at Leidsestraat, while men should head to the branch at Koningsplein 7. ☎ 626 79 93 ✉ Leidsestraat 10 ☽ 10am-6pm Mon-Sat (to 9pm Thu), 1-6pm Sun 🚊 1, 2, 5

CLOTHING & SHOE SIZES

Women's Clothing

Aust/UK	8	10	12	14	16	18
Europe	36	38	40	42	44	46
Japan	5	7	9	11	13	15
USA	6	8	10	12	14	16

Women's Shoes

Aust/USA	5	6	7	8	9	10
Europe	35	36	37	38	39	40
France only	35	36	38	39	40	42
Japan	22	23	24	25	26	27
UK	3½	4½	5½	6½	7½	8½

Men's Clothing

Aust	92	96	100	104	108	112
Europe	46	48	50	52	54	56

	S	M	M		L	
Japan						
UK/USA	35	36	37	38	39	40

Men's Shirts (Collar Sizes)

Aust/Japan	38	39	40	41	42	43
Europe	38	39	40	41	42	43
UK/USA	15	15½	16	16½	17	17½

Men's Shoes

Aust/ UK	7	8	9	10	11	12
Europe	41	42	43	44½	46	47
Japan	26	27	27.5	28	29	30
USA	7½	8½	9½	10½	11½	12½

Measurements are approximate only; try before you buy.

Van Ravenstein (5, C5)

Gerda van Ravenstein's impeccable selection showcases the best of Dries van Noten, Ann Demeule-meester and Dirk Bikkem-bergs, among others. Style hunters go for the clothes' understated elegance and pay handsomely for them. There's an itsy-bitsy bargain basement, too.

☎ 639 00 67 ✉ Keizers-gracht 359 ⊙ 1-6pm Mon, 11am-6pm Tue-Fri (to 7pm Thu), 10.30am-5pm Sat ⛟ 1, 2, 5, 13, 14, 17

STREET WEAR

Exota (2, A5)

Outfitting hipsters of both sexes, Exota is full of quality club clothes, hard-to-find street-wear labels and kooky giftware. Alternative labels such as Aem Kei and King Louie hang alongside better-known brands such as Kookai and French Connection.

☎ 620 91 02 ✉ Harten-straat 10 ⊙ 11am-6pm Mon, 10am-6pm Tue-Sat (to 9pm Thu), 1-5pm Sun ⛟ 1, 2, 5, 13, 14, 17

Ripper retro at Zipper

Henxs (2, E6)

For a small store, these skater dudes stock a huge range of brands. The usual suspects (Carhartt, Evisu and G-Star) are all here, along with a few rarer breeds. There's a great collection of street shoes and all manner of skate, hip-hop and graffiti magazines to peruse.

☎ 416 77 86 ✉ Sint Antoniesbreestraat 136 ⊙ 10am-6pm Tue-Sat, 1-6pm Sun & Mon ⛟ 9, 14 Ⓜ Nieuwmarkt

SECOND-HAND GEAR

Lady Day (2, A5)

The premier location for unearthing spotless vintage clothes. The leather jackets and woollen sailors' coats are well priced and perfect for freezing winter days, while the range of sportswear old-timers is hard to beat.

☎ 623 58 20 ✉ Harten-straat 9 ⊙ 11am-6pm Mon-Sat (to 9pm Thu), 1-6pm Sun ⛟ 1, 2, 5, 13, 14, 17

Laura Dols (2, A6)

After the Lana Turner look? You've come to the right place. Laura Dols is full of marvellous period pieces from the '40s and '50s, such as pristine satin dresses, fur-collared woollen coats and Bakelite handbags.

☎ 624 90 66 ✉ Wolvenstraat 6 & 7 ⊙ 11am-6pm Mon-Sat (to 9pm Thu), 2-6pm Sun ⛟ 1, 2, 5, 13, 14, 17

Zipper (2, E6)

Step into a time warp of nostalgic American vintage gear for funksters. Sift through a pricey but excellent range of jeans and customised club gear, kitschy Hawaiian shirts and '50s zoot suits. There's another equally good Zipper store at Huidenstraat 7.

☎ 627 03 53 ✉ Nieuwe Hoogstraat 8 ⊙ 11am-6pm Mon-Sat (to 9pm Thu), 1-5pm Sun ⛟ 9, 14 Ⓜ Nieuwmarkt

---

A Taxing Question

Value-added tax (VAT) of 19% is included in retail prices in the Netherlands. Visitors from non-EU countries are entitled to a refund on goods over €150 (if purchased from a single shop on one day and exported within three months). Ask for an export certificate when purchasing, then hand it to Dutch customs when you leave the Netherlands. The supplier will refund the tax to you by mail, or to your credit card.

Easier still is shopping at Tax Free for Tourists outlets (look out for the sticker), though they often sell tacky souvenirs rather than quality giftware. Keep in mind the world-renowned duty-free shopping at Schiphol airport.

ARTS & ANTIQUES

Boekie Woekie (5, C4)
It's hard to tell if Boekie Woekie is gallery, bookshop or a bit of both. Art lovers and bibliophiles head here for handmade books, prints, monographs and *objets d'art* by local and international artists.
☎ 639 05 07 ✉ Berenstraat 16 🕑 noon-6pm Mon-Fri, to 5pm Sat 🚊 1, 2, 5, 13, 14, 17

Decorativa (3, C1)
Decorativa gives the BBC props department a run for its money with its marble statues, oversized candlesticks, period costumes and crystal chandeliers crammed into every spare inch of space. The eccentric owner also does a roaring trade in European antiques and 17th- and 18th-century Dutch paintings.
☎ 320 10 93 ✉ Nieuwe Spiegelstraat 9A 🕑 noon-6pm Tue-Fri, 11am-5pm Sat 🚊 1, 2, 5, 7, 10, 16, 24, 25

Eduard Kramer (3, C1)
The friendly folk at Kramer leave the serious demeanour of antique dealing to the street's more sober dealers. Instead, this kooky family-run business is full to bursting with antique wall and floor tiles and vintage homewares (candlesticks, teapots, crystal decanters, semiprecious jewellery and pocket watches).
☎ 623 08 32 ✉ Nieuwe Spiegelstraat 64 🕑 10am-6pm Mon-Sat, noon-6pm Sun 🚊 1, 2, 5, 7, 10, 16, 24, 25

Craving crystal chandeliers? Head for Nieuwe Spiegelstraat

EH Ariëns Kappers (3, C2)
Stand below Empire-style chandeliers while perusing Dutch prints, etchings, engravings and maps (including topographical maps of the Netherlands) from the 17th to the 20th centuries. The impeccably polite and informed owners are only too happy to display and discuss their much-loved collection of Japanese woodblock prints too.
☎ 623 53 56 ✉ Nieuwe Spiegelstraat 32 🕑 11am-5pm Tue-Sun 🚊 1, 2, 5, 7, 10, 16, 24, 25

Roerende Zaken (2, A6)
All sorts of recent history washes up at this vintage store with a great range of second-hand design classics and never-out-of-the-box goodies that, in their day, obviously missed the mark. But in our retro-obsessed age, you'll wow your friends with such treasures as a translucent vintage telephone or a classic Yogi Bear doll.
☎ 683 21 52 ✉ Oude Spiegelstraat 5 🕑 1-6pm Thu & Fri, 1-5pm Sat, 2-5pm Sun 🚊 1, 2, 5, 6, 13, 14, 17

Nobody does Dutch portraiture better than Decorativa

MUSIC & BOOKS

The American Book Center (2, B7)

Four floors of English-language books from the USA ensure this ramshackle bookshop is always bustling. There's an excellent magazine section too.

☎ 625 55 37 ✉ Kalverstraat 185 ◷ 10am-8pm Mon-Sat (to 9pm Thu), 11am-6.30pm Sun 🚊 1, 2, 4, 5, 9, 16, 24, 25

Architectura & Natura (2, A4)

This exquisite bookshop, on one of the city's most charming canals, sells a huge range on architecture, landscape and art. A good percentage of titles is in English, although the extensive stock of design and coffee-table books is beautiful in any language.

☎ 623 61 86 ✉ Leliegracht 22 ◷ noon-6pm Mon, 9am-6pm Tue, to 6.30pm Wed-Fri, to 6pm Sat 🚊 13, 14, 17

Artimo A-Z (5, C4)

If this stylish and unpretentious art bookshop doesn't have the book or art magazine you're after, the helpful staff will know exactly where to find it.

☎ 625 33 44 ✉ Elandsgracht 8 ◷ 11am-6pm Mon-Tue, 9am-7pm Wed-Fri, 11am-6pm Sat 🚊 10, 17

Athenaeum (2, B7)

The favourite of Amsterdam intellectuals, this enormous bookshop lures academics, journalists and students. The separate newsagency

has the city's largest selection of international newspapers and magazines.

☎ 622 62 48 ✉ Spui 14-16 ◷ 11am-6pm Mon, 9.30am-6pm Tue-Sat (to 9pm Thu), noon-5.30pm Sun 🚊 1, 2, 5

Au Bout du Monde (2, A6)

Losing your religion? Find a new one at Au Bout du Monde, a nirvana of philosophical and religious titles. This subdued and elegant bookshop has everything from Buddha to Bhagwan, shamanism to Shinto, Tao to tarot.

Amsterdam by the Book

At the top of any reading list is renowned Dutch historian Geert Mak's *Amsterdam: A Brief Life of the City*, packed with ripping yarns about Amsterdam's founders. Almost as good is Simon Schama's *The Embarrassment of Riches*, focusing on the Dutch Golden Age. Deborah Moggach's historical fiction *Tulip Fever* gives a feel for the city in the 17th century when Rembrandt was at his peak and tulips were worth more than their weight in gold. More recently, Amsterdam author Harry Mulisch wrote *The Last Call* and *The Assault* about Dutch apathy during WWII, and Nicholas Freeling, author of *Love in Amsterdam*, created the 1970s Van der Valk detective series.

Athenaeum: a lure for the literati

☎ 625 13 97 ✉ Singel 313 ◷ 1-6pm Mon, 10am-6pm Tue-Sat 🚊 1, 2, 5

Blue Note (2, C4)

The shop for jazz lovers. A calm oasis in Centrum's craziness, Blue Note treats its customers with free espresso as they listen to Dutch, European and American jazz recordings. They also carry a small but well-chosen selection of acid jazz and dance.

☎ 428 10 29 ✉ Gravenstraat 12 ◷ 11am-7pm Mon-Sat, noon-5pm Sun 🚊 1, 2, 4, 5, 9, 13, 16, 17, 24, 25

Concerto (3, E2)
This ardently scruffy shop, spread over several buildings, carries the city's best selection of new and second-hand tunes. Spend hours sifting through the boxes of bargain vinyl, priced from €2.
☎ 623 52 28 ✉ Utrechtsestraat 52-60 🕙 10am-6pm Mon-Sat (to 9pm Thu), noon-6pm Sun 🚊 4

The English Bookshop (5, B4)
A great range of fiction and nonfiction titles, and a small but beautiful selection of magazines, is available at this welcoming bookstore. The staff's knowledge of new books is second to none.
☎ 626 42 30 ✉ Lauriergracht 71 🕙 10am-9pm Thu, to 6pm Fri-Sat, 11am-5pm Sun 🚊 7, 10, 13, 14, 17

Lambiek (2, A9)
Philosopher Friedrich Nietzsche wasn't the only one obsessed by Superman; Lambiek has been hoarding comics of the good and evil variety at its store since 1968. They say they're the world's oldest comic store, and you'd need to be Brainiac to dispute the claim.
☎ 626 75 43 🖳 www.lambiek.nl ✉ Kerkstraat 119 🕙 11am-6pm Mon-Fri, to 5pm Sat, 1-5pm Sun 🚊 1, 2, 5

Mendo (5, C4)
Find the slickest array in the land of architecture, design, advertising, photography and fashion books at Mendo. Attached to a local ad agency, the beautifully laid-out store is as much

gallery as bookshop, with a changing array of work on the walls by local artists and graphic designers.
☎ 612 12 16 ✉ Berenstraat 11 🕙 Wed-Fri noon-6pm, Sat & Sun to 5pm 🚊 13, 14, 17

Scheltema (2, A8)
The largest bookshop in town boasts six floors stuffed full of books and magazines. There's a huge selection of English-language books in every department, and a nifty café on the 1st floor.
☎ 523 14 11 ✉ Koningsplein 20 🕙 10am-6pm Mon-Sat (to 9pm Thu), noon-6pm Sun 🚊 1, 2, 5

Soul Food (2, C4)
The laid-back boys at Soul Food know their rap, R&B, house, garage, big beat and

Brazilian. As well as imported style and music magazines, there are turntables for budding DJs to play with.
☎ 428 61 30 ✉ Nieuwe Nieuwstraat 27c 🕙 1-6pm Mon, 11am-6pm Tue-Fri (to 9pm Thu), to 5pm Sat 🚊 1, 2, 4, 5, 9, 13, 16, 17, 24, 25

Sound of the Fifties (5, C6)
Feel like an extra in a Dutch version of Nick Hornby's *High Fidelity* while surveying the selection of '50s and '60s jazz, rock, R&B, soul, gospel and doo-wop (CDs and vinyl). It isn't cheap, but most records and sleeves are in perfect condition.
☎ 623 97 45 ✉ Prinsengracht 669 🕙 noon-6pm Tue-Sat, to 5pm Mon 🚊 1, 2, 5, 6, 7, 10

Hitting the mark: Architectura & Natura (p55)

FOOD & DRINK

Australian Homemade (2, B8)

Who knows how a Belgian company with stores in the Netherlands ended up with this name? When questioned, management mumbled something vague about Aboriginal Australia's purity and the purity of their ingredients. But who cares when the chocolates and ice cream are this good? Also at Leidsestraat 101.

✉ **Singel 437**
🕑 10.30am-10pm Tue-Sat, noon-10pm Sun & Mon 🚋 1, 2, 5

De Belly (5, B2)

Anaemic sandal-wearers and visions of wholesome beauty alike flock to this organic supermarket from right around Amsterdam, because they know the tasty vegetables, melt-in-your-mouth chocolates and sourdough bread are worth crossing town for.

☎ 330 94 83 ✉ **Nieuwe Leliestraat 174**
🕑 8.30am-6.30pm Mon-Fri, to 5.30pm Sat 🚋 13, 14, 17

De Kaaskamer (5, C5)

The best cheese shop in town, and that's a big call for a nation that eats, on average, 12kg per person a year.

Better than home-made: Australian Homemade

If it's not busy, the owners may let you sample cheeses from all over Europe.

☎ 623 34 83
✉ **Runstraat 7** 🕑 noon-6pm Mon, 9am-6pm Tue-Fri, to 5pm Sat, noon-5pm Sun 🚋 1, 2, 5

Eichholtz (2, A8)

Its corner-store vibe is in keeping with the Little Piece of Home that expats find here: Americans come to stock up on chocolate-chip cookies, Brits their Lea & Perrins Worcestershire sauce. Eichholtz also stocks a fine selection of Dutch cheeses, chocolates and baked goods.

☎ 622 03 05
✉ **Leidsestraat 48**
🕑 10am-6pm Mon-Sat, 1-5pm Sun 🚋 1, 2, 5

Geels & Co (2, D4)

Sleazy Warmoesstraat is home to the distinguished Geels & Co, which for 140 years has been roasting coffee and vending loose tea. They also sell teapots, coffee plungers and other beverage-brewing gadgets. If visiting on a Saturday, look at the interesting museum upstairs.

☎ 624 06 83
✉ **Warmoesstraat 67**
🕑 9.30am-6pm Mon-Sat
🚋 4, 9, 16, 24, 25

Le Cellier (2, B4)

All manner of spirits, *genevers* (Dutch gin) and liqueurs are represented here. Standout selections of grappa and rum are augmented by a large assortment of New World wines and over 75 beers.

☎ 638 65 73 ✉ **Spuistraat 116** 🕑 11am-6pm Mon, 9.30am-6pm Tue-Fri, to 5.30pm Sat
🚋 1, 2, 5, 13, 17

Puccini Bomboni (2, A4)

This purveyor of huge, handmade and utterly indulgent chocolate bonbons gets chocoholics salivating. Treat your sweet tooth to the unforgettable Calvados chocolate cup.

☎ 427 83 41 ✉ **Singel 184** 🕑 11am-6pm Tue-Sat, noon-5pm Sun
🚋 1, 2, 5, 13, 17

Good to the Last Scrape

No domestic item represents Dutch thrift better than the *flessenlikker* (bottle-scraper), a device widely used only in Holland. This miracle tool can tempt those last elusive smears from a mayonnaise jar or salad-dressing bottle. They're available in most homeware shops.

FOR CHILDREN

Bam Bam (2, B4)
Pampered little princes and princesses get dressed head to toe in Bam Bam's designer clothes. On the dramatic top floor of Magna Plaza, Amsterdam's bubba store for parents with too much money is in the former cafeteria.
☎ 624 52 15 ✉ Magna Plaza ⏱ 11am-7pm Mon, 10am-7pm Tue-Sat (to 9pm Thu), noon-7pm Sun 🚊 1, 2, 5, 13, 17

Exota Kids (5, C2)
Hip parents retain their cool quota by cladding their kids in Exota Kids. Top picks include crocheted beanies, denim overalls, polar-fleece skirts or anything by Exota's own label, Petit Louie.
☎ 420 68 84 ✉ Nieuwe Leliestraat 32 ⏱ 11am-6pm Mon, 10am-6pm Tue-Sat, 1-5pm Sun 🚊 13, 14, 17

Kitsch Kitchen Kids (5, B3)
Looking like a props shop for a South American festival, Kitsch Kitchen Kids (not a front for the Klan) is a riot of colour and high tack for the little tackers. Be prepared to spend up big on crazy Mexican toys, over-the-top dress-ups and plastic-fantastic furniture.
☎ 622 82 61 ✉ Rozengracht 183 ⏱ 10am-6pm Mon-Sat 🚊 13, 14, 17

Mechanisch Speelgoed (5, C1)
Get in touch with your inner child at Mechanisch Speelgoed. It's crammed full of nostalgic and wind-up toys, snow domes, glow lamps, finger puppets and pull-along toys of every conceivable description.
☎ 638 16 80 ✉ Westerstraat 67 ⏱ 10am-6pm Mon, Tue, Thu & Fri, to 5pm Sat 🚊 3, 10

Oilily (3, B3)
For kids' clothes you'll wish you could wear, check out Oilily's fun, colourful range. Always wanted rattle-toe socks, a floppy-ear beanie or flying-pigtail sweatshirt? This is the place.
☎ 672 33 61 ✉ PC Hooftstraat 131-133 ⏱ 1-6pm Mon, 10am-6pm Tue & Wed, to 9pm Thu, to 6.30pm Fri, 5pm Sat, noon-5pm Sun 🚊 2, 3, 5, 12

Pinokkio (2, B4)
Forget doll's houses – they're *so* 20th century. Get with the program and buy the little tykes a handmade wooden Dutch canal house (€110). Too bulky? Small items (mobiles, Pinocchio dolls, music boxes) are almost as good.
☎ 622 89 14 ✉ Magna Plaza ⏱ 11am-7pm Mon, 10am-7pm Tue-Sat (to 9pm Thu), noon-7pm Sun 🚊 1, 2, 5, 13, 17

Confounded by choice at Kitsch Kitchen Kids

SPECIALIST STORES

Big Shoe (2, A4)
You know what they say about big feet? They need big shoes. The large-hoofed are so often denied up-to-the-minute shoe styles. Here, though, are big shoes for big feet (sizes 13 to 20 US), in styles usually available only in the normal range.
☎ 622 66 45 ✉ Leliegracht 12 ⏱ 10am-5pm Tue-Sat (to 9pm Thu) 🚊 1, 2, 5, 13, 14, 17

Brilmuseum (2, A5)
The Glasses Museum is a must-see for four-eyed folk. It turns eyewear into a fetish, and most of the thousands of vintage frames are for sale. They also sell decidedly hip-to-the-groove modern frames.
☎ 421 24 14 ✉ Gasthuismolensteeg 7 ⏱ 11.30am-5.30pm Wed-Fri, to 5pm Sat 🚊 1, 2, 5, 13, 14, 17

De Witte Tanden Winkel (5, C5)
Amsterdam caters to every fetish, so why not teeth? The White Teeth Store stocks over 150 styles of toothbrush, including Hello Kitty, Star Wars

De Witte Tanden Winkel – your teething troubles are over

MARTIN MOOS

and Bugs Bunny scrubbers. And there's every tooth-care accessory imaginable, including everyone's favourite: roasted-aubergine–flavoured toothpaste.
☎ 623 34 43 ✉ Runstraat 5 ⏱ 1-6pm Mon, 10am-6pm Tue-Fri, to 5pm Sat 🚊 1, 2, 5

Frozen Fountain (5, C5)
Amsterdam's premier showcase of furniture and interior design is the place for big spending on offbeat, hypercool custom furniture (local and international), or to pick up little knick-knacks such as designer penknives

and coffee pots you'll always remember you bought here.
☎ 622 93 75 ✉ Prinsengracht 629 ⏱ 1-6pm Mon, 10am-6pm Tue-Fri, to 5pm Sat 🚊 7, 10

Kitsch Kitchen (5, C3)
Transform your home into a colourful temple of kitsch with wacky Mexican tablecloths, pink plastic chandeliers from India and printed sheet-metal furniture from Ghana. The owners' decorating credo is simple: too much colour and tackiness ain't ever enough!
☎ 428 49 69 ✉ Bloemdwarsstraat 21 ⏱ 10am-6pm Mon-Sat 🚊 13, 14, 17

Delftware
Delftware (earthenware pottery covered with a lustrous tin-oxide glaze) was created as imitation Ming dynasty porcelain. Developed in the early 1600s, the collectibles depict windmills, birds or flowers in blue and white while other pieces are in vivid red, green and gold. Many shops carry a good range of royal, antique and modern delftware, but three of the best are:
- **Galleria d'Arte Rinascimento** (5, C2; ☎ 622 75 09, Prinsengracht 170; ⏱ 9.30am-6pm)
- **Heinen** (5, C6; ☎ 627 82 99; Prinsengracht 440; ⏱ 10am-6pm Mon-Sat)
- **Hogendoorn & Kaufman** (2, B7; ☎ 638 27 36; Rokin 124; ⏱ 10am-6pm Mon-Sat, to 9pm Thu, 1-5pm Sun)

Nieuws (5, C3)

Nieuws specialises in quirky trinkets. The owner does a great job of sourcing the deeply ironic, from Sigmund Freud action figures ('Sometimes a cigar is just a cigar') to the Pimp Daddy body wash (with babe activator).

☎ 627 95 40
✉ Prinsengracht 297
🕙 1-6.30pm Mon, 10am-6.30pm Tue-Fri, 11am-6pm Sat & Sun
🚃 1, 2, 5, 13, 14, 17

PGC Hajenius (2, B7)

The Art Deco interior of this renowned tobacco emporium is too grand, and the products and paraphernalia – including traditional leaf cigars, clay pipes and humidors – far too interesting, for any of it to be good for you.

☎ 623 74 94 ✉ Rokin 92 🕙 noon-6pm Mon, 10am-6pm Tue-Sat (to 8pm Thu), noon-5pm Sun
🚃 4, 9, 16, 20, 24, 25

Santa Jet (2, A2)

Relationship a bit rocky? Career in the doldrums? Hotfoot it to Santa Jet and buy up big. All you need is their funky prayer candles and love potions, a few Mexican shrines and religious icons, some Day of the Dead knickknacks and an assortment of good-luck charms.

☎ 427 20 70 ✉ Prinsenstraat 7 🕙 11am-6pm Mon-Fri, 10am-5pm Sat, noon-5pm Sun 🚃 1, 2, 5, 13, 17

Vivian Hann (1, D2)

Most homeware stores suck because they're filled with chrome espresso cups and overpriced toilet brushes. Vivian Hann's is different: sure, the price on the odd plate could feed a Bangladeshi village for six months, but many of the exquisitely original products are quite affordable.

☎ 06-220 49 465
✉ Haarlemmerdijk 102
🕙 11am-5.30pm Wed-Fri, 10.30am-5pm Sat
🚃 1, 2, 3, 5, 13, 17

Coster Diamonds – more tempting than Tiffany's

RICHARD NEBESKY

Top of the Rocks

The Netherlands has been a big name in the diamond world since Jewish diamond cutters, fleeing persecution in Antwerp, settled here in 1585. Some of the most precious stones ever found have been processed in Amsterdam: the largest, Cullinan (3106 carats), was split into over 100 stones, and the smallest (0.00012 carat) was also cut here.

Today, the city has a dozen diamond factories where prices are competitive, but not necessarily cheaper than at retail shops. They'll rejoice at an opportunity to show you their stock. Some of the more established ones are:

- **Amsterdam Diamond Center** (2, C5; ☎ 624 57 87; Rokin 1-5; 🕙 10am-6pm Mon-Sat, 11am-6pm Sun; 🚃 4, 9, 16, 24, 25)
- **Coster Diamonds** (3, B3; ☎ 305 55 55; Paulus Potterstraat 2-6; 🕙 9am-5pm; 🚃 2, 3, 5)
- **Van Moppes & Zoon** (3, C4; ☎ 676 12 42; Albert Cuypstraat 2-6; 🕙 9am-5.30pm; 🚃 16, 24, 25)

RECREATIONAL DRUGS

Smart drug shops started popping up all over the city in the early 1990s and are now an established addition to the coffeeshop scene (p93). They sell legal, organic hallucinogens such as magic mushrooms, herbal joints and ecstasy, seeds (opium, marijuana, psychoactive), mood enhancers and aphrodisiacs.

Welcome to Amsterdam, Have a Nice Trip!

It's legal to sell fresh magic mushrooms over the counter in Amsterdam because the Dutch Ministry of Health has found they're not hazardous when used responsibly – heed their warning. Before you make a purchase, ask the staff to explain what dosage to consume and what to expect from your 'trip'. Warning: the same fungal products are probably illegal to take back home.

Chills & Thrills (2, C2)

The city's most commercial smart shop is always packed full of tourists trying to hear each other over the dance music. On sale are herbal trips, mushrooms, psychoactive cacti, amino-acid drinks, novelty bongs and that dope-fiend status symbol of choice, the life-size alien sculpture. ☎ 638 00 15 ✉ Nieuwendijk 17 ☼ 11am-9pm 🚋 1, 2, 5, 13, 17

Dream Lounge (3, C1)

Enhance your mind, mood and libido at Amsterdam's original smart shop. The knowledgeable staff will happily explain the effects of the various magic mushrooms, mood powders and other drugs and stimulants on sale. ☎ 626 69 07 ✉ Kerkstraat 93 ☼ 11am-7pm Mon-Wed, to 8pm Thu-Sat, noon-5pm Sun 🚋 1, 2, 5

Kokopelli (2, D3)

This huge store in the red-light district sells a variety of mushrooms, smart drugs and dope paraphernalia. If you're with your beloved, purchase some sex stimulants and spend the evening staring wistfully into each others' eyes. There's also beginners' bondage kits if things get really serious. ☎ 421 70 00 ✉ Warmoesstraat 12 ☼ 11am-10pm 🚋 4, 9, 16, 24, 25

Magic Mushroom Gallery (2, B6)

With so many varieties of fresh magic mushrooms on sale (€12.50 to €17.50), it's a good thing the demonstrative staff know what the likely effects on your delicate psyche will be. ☎ 427 57 65 ✉ Spuistraat 249 ☼ 11am-10pm Sun-Thu 🚋 1, 2, 5, 13, 17

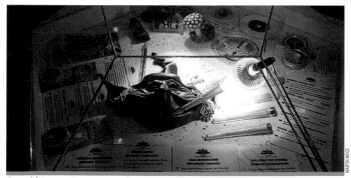

Fungal fever: get into some mind games at the Magic Mushroom Gallery

SEX SHOPS

If you've never been into a sex shop, Amsterdam is the place to start. While many shops are sleazy affairs staffed by creepy characters, there are also wonderful stores where the charming and enthusiastic staff can help you choose something that could make life that little bit more fun.

Absolute Danny (2, D5)
Acclaimed by Dutch *Playboy* as Amsterdam's classiest sex shop, Absolute Danny was the first in the city to be run by a woman, making the atmosphere distinctly different from most. It veers towards fetish clothing, including rubber lingerie, PVC, leather and corsets. There's also tasteful hard-core videos and dildos – the highlight being the Tarzan model.
☎ 421 09 15 ✉ Oudezijds Achterburgwal 78 ⏰ noon-8pm Mon-Sat (to 9pm Thu), to 7pm Sun 🚊 4, 9, 16, 24, 25

Female & Partners (2, B4)
This classy shop draws in all types, from young single women to middle-aged

Risqué business in Amsterdam

couples. There's a huge range of erotic underwear, sensible sex toys (there's not a triple-ended, 16-inch dildo in sight) and videos that many women will prefer to what's on offer elsewhere.
☎ 620 9152 ✉ Spuistraat 100 ⏰ 1-6pm Mon, 11am-6pm Tue-Sun (to 9pm Thu) 🚊 1, 2, 5, 13, 17

Mr B (2, D4)
This trashy leather and rubber store kits out adventurous gay lads with outfits for every occasion. There's also a vast selection of videos, and an equally sizable range of toys on the walls that can only be described as well hung.
☎ 422 00 03 ✉ Warmoesstraat 89 ⏰ noon-6pm 🚊 4, 9, 16, 24, 25

Whether it's latex, leather or PVC, Female & Partners has it covered

Eating

Let's face it, in the culinary world Dutch cuisine is pretty close to the bottom of the food chain. Concentrating on filling the stomach rather than titillating the taste buds, the Dutch have a national cuisine based on a rudimentary meat, potato and vegetable theme. That said, there's an increasing number of places doing tasty variations on staid old Dutch dishes. And virtually every other cuisine is represented in Amsterdam, from sophisticated French to spicy Surinamese.

The city's most interesting eateries are dotted along the many side streets inside the canal belt and in the Jordaan and Nieuwmarkt neighbourhoods. Don't overlook the many lively brown cafés, grand cafés and bars that also serve excellent meals (p80).

If you want to do some planning, www.specialbite.com gives a great rundown of the hippest and most happening eateries in Amsterdam.

Some restaurants list a dish of the day (*dagschotel*) or set menu (*dagmenu*); look out for these, as they are often great value, though they'll probably offer little in the way of culinary adventure.

Meal Costs

The price ranges used in this chapter indicate the cost of a main course for one person.

€   under €8
€€   €9-15
€€€   €16-25
€€€€   over €25

Dining alfresco in Amsterdam

Dinner is eaten early in Holland, with most restaurant kitchens open from 5.30pm to 10pm only, though diners are welcome to linger over a drink long after food service finishes at most restaurants. Opening hours, rather than food service times, are listed in this guide.

You can't just become a brown café overnight; it takes years of cigarette smoke to achieve the right shade of staining

CENTRUM: OLD SIDE

1e Klas (2, E2) €€€
French
Once reserved for first-class passengers only, this elegant restaurant at Centraal Station has been thrown open to the hoi polloi. There's an abundance of 19th-century splendour, with a monumental Art Nouveau bar, etched mirrors and tall porcelain vases.
☎ 625 01 31 ✉ Platform 2b, Centraal Station
☼ 8.30am-11pm
🚊 Centraal Station
♿ excellent 🚻 Ⓥ

Brasserie Harkema (2, C6) €€
International
This über-hip restaurant in an old tobacco factory opened to grand hurrahs of appreciation from locals, impressed by its grand sense of space and classy international menu. The wonderful meals, which range from fine-dining fish to hamburgers, are surprisingly cheap (€5 to €12), and the kitchen stays open till 11pm most nights.
☎ 428 22 22 ✉ Nes 67
☼ 11am-1am (to 3am Fri & Sat) 🚊 4, 9, 16, 24, 25

De Waag: once a witch weigh station, now a charming café

Café de Jaren (2, C7) €€
International
One of the city's truly grand cafés. Light floods in through the huge windows of this old bank, making for a special daytime buzz. There's also a glow provided by the beautiful staff and clientele. They get the *Guardian* and the *International Herald-Tribune* daily and, on a sunny afternoon, the café's pristine canalside terrace is one of Amsterdam's magical spots.
☎ 625 57 71 ✉ Nieuwe Doelenstraat 20
☼ 10am-1am 🚊 4, 9, 14, 16, 24, 25 ♿ excellent
🚻 Ⓥ

Cafe in de Waag (2, E5) €€€
International
De Waag has had many incarnations (p31); merchants brought produce here to be taxed, and women were weighed to determine if they were witches. These days the only anguish you'll encounter is deciding which dish to order from the extensive menu. On sunny days, the outside terrace is a popular place to watch the market crowds.
☎ 422 77 72 ✉ Nieuwmarkt 4 ☼ 10am-1am
🚊 4, 9, 16, 24, 25
Ⓜ Nieuwmarkt ♿ fair
🚻 Ⓥ

Paying the Bill
Meal prices are reasonable by European standards and servings are large – the Dutch love a hearty feed. A service charge of 15% is usually included in the bill, and locals round off to the nearest euro or give a 5% to 10% tip, depending on the service. As you settle the bill, the protocol is to say how much you're paying and to leave the tip in cash rather than on the credit-card slip. Reservations are often wise (see individual listings), and many smaller restaurants don't accept credit cards.

Chang Express (2, E3) €
Asian
A no-frills eatery that serves up intimidatingly large plates of Asian food, ranging from Chinese and Vietnamese to Indian — hell, there's even some Surinamese thrown in for good measure. It's not glamorous, but it's a great place to stop for a quick bite before exploring the red-light district.
☎ 620 30 08 ⊠ Nieuweburdsteeg 14-16 ☒ noon-10pm 🚋 4, 9, 16, 24, 25 🚇 Centraal Station ♿ fair ♿ Ⓥ

Dantzig (2, E7) €€
International
Next to the Stopera, Dantzig is constantly busy feeding thespians and theatregoers from its eclectic snack and meals menu. Unwind after a visit to Waterlooplein flea market on the sprawling riverside terrace — boasting beautiful views over the Amstel — and order their classic club sandwich, piled as high as it is wide.
☎ 620 90 39 ⊠ Zwanenburgwal 15 ☒ 9am-1am Mon-Thu (to 2am Fri & Sat), 10am-11pm Sun 🚋 4, 9, 14 ♿ good ♿ Ⓥ

Hemelse Modder (2, F5) €€€
International
Hemelse Modder has worked out the elusive secret of ongoing restaurant success. First, create a beautifully decorated restaurant (floor-to-ceiling mauve velvet curtains, well-spaced tables and displays of dramatic tropical flowers). Then conceive a menu of palate-pleasing dishes at less than upmarket prices (three-course set meal €26, five-course €32).
☎ 624 32 03 ⊠ Oude Waal 11 ☒ 6-10pm Tue-Sun 🚇 Nieuwmarkt ♿ good Ⓥ

Inez IPSC (2, C8) €€€
Fusion
With its anonymous entrance, Inez IPSC (International Private Society Club) hides its love away to dissuade the casual diner: they only want those in the know. Diners are rewarded for their insider knowledge with fabulous fusion food in an audacious pink-and-green dining room offering

Veg Out
Vegetarians are well catered for in Amsterdam, with most menus featuring at least a couple of meat-free options. There are also several specialist vegetarian restaurants, including the following:

- De Bolhoed (p69)
- Deshima Proeflokaal (p72)
- De Vilegende Schotel (☎ 625 20 41; Nieuwe Leliestraat 162) A comfortable place that also does vegan dishes.

MARTIN MOOS

Voraciously vegetarian: De Bolhoed (p69)

Raan Phad Thai – one visit and you'll be running back for more

great views of Muntplein. Bookings are essential.
☎ 639 28 99 ✉ 1st fl, Amstel ⏰ 7pm-midnight 🚋 4, 9, 14, 16, 24, 25 ♿ fair

Latei (2, E5) €
International
Loveable Latei is the Zeedijk at its most eccentric. Purveyor of the area's best coffee, fluffy, flavoursome omelettes and delectable sandwiches, Latei also sells high-quality Finnish wallpaper, olive oil from Umbria and all manner of 1950s objects, including lamps and trinkets. At night, it does a healthy couscous salad (€6) that vegetarians will love.
☎ 625 74 85 ✉ Zeedijk 143 ⏰ 8am-6pm Mon-Wed, to 10pm Thu-Fri, 9am-10pm Sat, 11am-6pm Sun Ⓜ Nieuwmarkt ♿ fair 🚻 Ⓥ

Puccini (2, D7) €€
Italian
After Waterlooplein market, refuel at this stylish café on the canal nearby. The fresh and healthy sandwiches and salads are bursting with sun-dried ingredients, while the apple strudel washed down with coffee is a victory for humanity. They also do pre-theatre meals until 8pm when there's a concert at the Stopera.
☎ 620 84 58 ✉ Staalstraat 21 ⏰ 8.30am-6pm Mon-Fri, 10am-6pm Sat & Sun 🚋 4, 9, 16, 24, 25 ♿ good 🚻 Ⓥ

Raan Phad Thai (2, D5) €
Thai
This tiny restaurant on Nieuwmarkt, like a scene from a Marx Bros film, always seems to be able to fit more people in. The cheery ladies cooking the Thai fare – the green curry is superb – often shuffle customers to make way for new arrivals, and it's great fun seeing which diners will crack when asked to shift over for the seventh time.
☎ 420 06 65 ✉ Kloveniersburgwal 18 ⏰ 2-10pm Ⓜ Nieuwmarkt ♿ poor 🚻 Ⓥ

Comfort Cuisine
Some traditional Dutch dishes include:
Appelgebak Warm apple pie with whipped cream.
Erwentsoep Thick pea soup with smoked sausage and bacon.
Kroketten Crumbed, deep-fried meat or shrimp-filled croquettes, served with mustard.
Pannenkoeken Large pancakes with ingredients such as bacon and cheese or apples and cherries.
Uitsmijter Fried eggs, ham and cheese on toast.

Raap & Peper (4, A4) €€€
Mediterranean
It started life as the communal kitchen of a well-known Amsterdam squat, and this out-of-the-way restaurant is now well known for its romantic fine dining, dark-wood interior, candles and crisp white linen. The food is equally classy, with duck and fish their specialities. It's popular with lesbians, especially for wedding banquets.
☎ 330 17 16 ✉ Peperstraat 23-25 ⏱ 6-11pm Tue-Sun 🚌 22, 32, 33, 34, 35 ♿ fair Ⓥ

Supper Club (2, B5) €€€€
International
Wine, dine and recline at the Supper Club, an Amsterdam institution that may be taking the piss ever so slightly. The interior is transformed nightly according to the cuisine; one night it might be downtown Naples (with laundry hanging from the ceiling), the next a sophisticated Paris salon. Bookings are advisable.
☎ 638 05 13 ✉ Jonge Roelensteeg 21 ⏱ 8pm-1am Wed-Sat 🚊 1, 2, 5, 13, 17 ♿ poor Ⓥ

Tisfris (2, E6) €€
Café
Brimming with good cheer, this place is packed with a mix of creative locals, lunching mums and shoppers stopping in after rummaging through stalls at the nearby Waterlooplein flea market. Its affable staff serve up scrumptious, healthy meals, salads and sandwiches, and it gets flooded with morning sun, making it ideal for breakfast. The canalside terrace is also a winner on sunny days.
☎ 622 04 72 ✉ Sint Antoniesbreestraat 142 ⏱ 9am-7pm 🚊 9, 14 Ⓜ Nieuwmarkt ♿ poor 🏳 Ⓥ

Best Terraces in Town
- Café de Jaren (p64)
- De Sluyswacht (p85)
- Tisfris (above)
- 't Smalle (p82)

Where better to fritter away the day than at Tisfris?

CENTRUM: NEW SIDE

Suffering from postpurchase syndrome? Revive your spirits at Caffè Esprit

Caffè Esprit (2, B7)   €€
American
Watch pretty girls and boys sipping their decaf macchiatos while they confront postpurchase doubts. They're comforted by the colossal club sandwiches and larger-than-life salads.
☎ 622 19 67 ✉ Spui 10
🕙 10am-6pm Mon-Sat (to 10pm Thu), noon-6pm Sun 🚊 1, 2, 4, 5, 9, 16, 24, 25 ♿ excellent ♿ Ⓥ

Dorrius (2, D3)   €€€
Dutch
Long established and well loved, Dorrius soothes its customers with convivial service and faultless cooking. Dressed-up diners come here to cut deals and celebrate special occasions. The atmospheric olde-worlde interior (marble floor, leather wallpaper, velvet upholstered chairs) is a classic backdrop for traditional Dutch dishes.
☎ 420 22 24 ✉ Nieuwezijds Voorburgwal 5
🕙 6pm-midnight 🚊 1, 2, 5, 13, 17 ♿ fair

d'Vijff Vlieghen Restaurant (2, A7)   €€€
Dutch
Spread out over five 17th-century canal houses,

d'Vijff Vlieghen is a glorious dining experience. Ask to be seated in the Rembrandt Room (which has four original etchings by the master) and join other splurging foreigners and businesspeople being treated to silver service and chi-chi Dutch food. Book ahead.
☎ 530 40 60
✉ Spuistraat 294-302
🕙 5.30-10.30pm
🚊 1, 2, 5 ♿ good
♿ Ⓥ

Green Planet (2, B4)   €€
Vegetarian
A modern veggie eatery that cares: about your health, biodegradable packaging and the food coming from its busy kitchen. On offer are soups, salads, antipasti and a hotchpotch of international dishes such as goulash and Indian curries.
☎ 625 82 80 ✉ Spuistraat 122 🕙 5.30-10.30pm Wed-Sun
🚊 1, 2, 5, 13, 17
♿ excellent ♿ Ⓥ

Pannenkoekenhuis (2, C7)   €
Dutch
Climb some of Amsterdam's steepest stairs to reach this tiny restaurant serving pancakes the likes of which you're not likely to have seen at home. The bacon, cheese and ginger pancake is a favourite. It's a one-man show, so service operates at a leisurely pace.
☎ 626 56 03 ✉ Grimburgwal 2 🕙 noon-4pm
🚊 4, 9, 16, 24, 25
♿ poor ♿ Ⓥ

If Eating Is Your Business
If you're in Amsterdam to wheel and deal with the captains of industry, some of the most impressive restaurants for schmoozing are:

- Christophe (p75)
- Dorrius (above)
- La Rive (p72)
- d'Vijff Vlieghen Restaurant (above)
- Zuid Zeeland (p77)

JORDAAN

Bordewijk (2, A1)   €€€
French
Bordewijk's interior is so minimal there's nought to do but appreciate the spectacular French cooking and snooty staff, the spartan décor doesn't do wonders for the acoustics but you'll be too busy yelling about the delectable fare to notice the din. In summer book a table at their idyllic canalside terrace on the Noordermarkt.
☎ 624 38 99 ⊠ Noordermarkt 7 ⏱ 7-11pm Tue-Sun 🚊 1, 2, 5, 13, 17 ♿ excellent Ⓥ

Café Reibach (2, A1)   €€
Breakfast & Lunch
Start your day at this charming canalside café that serves magnificent breakfast platters laden with Dutch cheese, pâté, smoked salmon, eggs, coffee and fresh juice. Afternoon tea is just as impressive.
☎ 626 77 08 ⊠ Brouwersgracht 139 ⏱ 10am-6pm 🚊 1, 2, 5, 13, 17 ♿ fair 👶 Ⓥ

De Belhamel (2, B1)   €€
International
De Belhamel's décor is so sumptuous, the staff could plate up raw onions and customers would still keep coming. Fortunately, the chef cares as much about the food as the gorgeous Art Nouveau interior. Expect Dutch twists on French and Italian classics. Book ahead.
☎ 622 10 95 ⊠ Brouwersgracht 60 ⏱ 6-10pm 🚊 1, 2, 5, 13, 17 ♿ fair Ⓥ

De Bolhoed (2, A2)   €€
Vegetarian
At the most popular vegetarian restaurant in town, fresh-faced waiters actually smile as they serve up an international menu of organic food. You'll find it hard to choose between the wide range of Italian, Mexican and Middle Eastern dishes. If you can't decide, make like a local: snag a seat on the terrace and order the banana-cream pie, served here for more than 18 years.
☎ 626 18 03 ⊠ Prinsengracht 60-62 ⏱ noon-10pm (from 11am on Saturday) 🚊 13, 14, 17 ♿ excellent 👶 Ⓥ

Duende (2, A1)   €
Spanish
Flamenco music, shared tables and delectable tapas (€3 to €6 per dish) guarantee Duende's popularity, even if the busy bar means slow service. But the Andalusian food really is top-notch; tuck into the huge shrimps with garlic, fried squid rings and mini-Spanish omelettes or, if you really need a pep up, a serve of bulls' testicles. ¡Ole!
☎ 420 66 92 ⊠ Lindengracht 62 ⏱ 4pm-1am Mon-Thu, to 3am Fri & Sat, 2pm-1am Sun 🚊 1, 2, 5, 13, 17 ♿ good 👶 Ⓥ

Lof (2, C1)   €€€€
Fusion
A few years back, Lof pioneered fusion food in Amsterdam, and is still combining east Asian and Mediterranean flavours with perfection. Your two options are a three-/five-course set menu costing €32.50/42.50; for fare this good, this is a bargain. Bookings are essential.
☎ 620 29 97 ⊠ Haarlemmerstraat 62 ⏱ 7-11pm Tue-Sun 🚊 1, 2, 5, 13, 17 ♿ good Ⓥ

Café Reibach: tiny in size but big on breakfast

Moeder's Pot Eethuisje (1, B1) €
Dutch

This gorgeously kitsch place ladles up honest, unfussy Dutch fare of the meat-and-three-veg variety. It's been dishing it out for 30 years, which is probably how long it's been since they last cleared out the clutter that dominates every inch of this restaurant, including the ceiling. Dig the cherub above the counter.

☎ 623 76 43 ✉ Vinkenstraat 119 🕙 5.30-9.30pm Mon-Sat 🚊 1, 2, 3, 5, 13, 17 ♿ excellent ♿

NOA (5, C6) €€€
Asian

Noodles of Amsterdam cooks delectable – wait for it – noodles, with fabulous flavours from all over Asia. It's a seriously slick lounge set-up, geared towards the 'Hi, How Are You' crowd (note the lack of a question mark there) who want to be seen slurping noodles with folk as glam as themselves.

☎ 626 08 02 ✉ Leidsegracht 84 🕙 6pm-midnight Mon-Sat, from

1pm Sun 🚊 1, 2, 5, 7, 10 ♿ excellent **V**

Oranjerie (1, B1) €
Dutch

Want a brown café that doubles as the perfect local eatery? Here it is. Savoury meat-and-three-veg mains (€8 to €10), super professional bar staff and the overall good cheer of the clientele make this a special place. On cold days, grab the heated bench between the bar and front window.

☎ 624 82 68 ✉ Binnen Oranjestraat 22 🕙 4pm-1am (to 3am Fri & Sat) 🚊 1, 2, 5, 13, 17 ♿ fair ♿

Pathum Thai (1, B1) €€
Thai

Tucked away in a quiet backstreet is this relaxed, friendly Thai restaurant. The nightly crowds filling its tables come for Thai food as spicy and well prepared as any in the city, served by devoted staff.

☎ 624 49 36 ✉ Willemsstraat 16 🕙 5-10pm (closed Tuesday) 🚊 1, 2, 5, 13, 17 ♿ excellent ♿ **V**

Small World Catering (1, D2) €
Snacks

Food lovers flock to this tiny café for its über-gourmet salads and sandwiches made from the freshest ingredients. The store started life as a catering business, but such was the demand for the Australian owner's fab food that he opened the store for foodies who know their nosh. Come for their speciality, the goat's-cheese quiche, and the great coffee.

☎ 420 27 74 ✉ Binnen Oranjestraat 14 🕙 10.30am-8pm Tue-Sat, noon-8pm Sun 🚊 1, 2, 5, 13, 17 ♿ excellent

Toscanini (5, C1) €€€
Italian

Can't afford to rent that Tuscan villa this year? Toscanini's is the next best thing. The restaurant, a covered courtyard with an open kitchen, is the cinematic setting for classic Italian dishes, including the best minestrone this side of Milan. Reservations are essential.

☎ 623 28 13 ✉ Lindengracht 75 🕙 6-10.30pm 🚊 3, 10 ♿ fair

Worth a Trip

The dramatic **Cafe-Restaurant Amsterdam** (1, C2; ☎ 682 26 66; Watertorenplein 6 near Westergasfabriek; €€; 🕙 11am-1am, to 2am Fri & Sat; 🚊 10), 15 minutes' walk northwest of Jordaan, gets no points for an original name, but huge points for its unique surrounds. In the engine room of a disused pumping station, it attracts groups who want a hearty feed and room to move – including many mums juggling several small children, a mobile phone and a martini. The vast space is impressive, with its 100ft wooden ceiling featuring 22 floodlights rescued from the former Ajax and Olympic stadiums.

MARTIN MOOS

DE PIJP

De Ondeugd (3, D3) €€€
French
The Naughty One has French fare and fun-loving staff who are always ready to encourage good cheer. Weekends see a younger crowd propping up the bar while waiting for a table; the rest of the week it's more subdued. The food is reliably good.
☎ 672 06 51
✉ Ferdinand Bolstraat 13 ⏰ 6-11pm 🚋 24, 25 ♿ good Ⓥ

De Taart van m'n Tante (3, D3) €
Coffee & Cake
The pink flamingos out front are the first sign that something's up at this wonderful cake-and-coffee corner café. A glance at the window filled with the wildly coloured cakes confirms it, but a closer inspection is in order: those aren't classical wedding figurines topping the cakes. They might just

be garter-clad schoolgirls with more than a nipple exposed, or some S&M leather boys getting busy with a whip.
☎ 776 46 00
✉ Ferdinand Bolstraat 10 ⏰ 10am-6pm 🚋 3, 12, 16, 24, 25 ♿ excellent ♿ Ⓥ

Le Garage (3, B4) €€€
French
Eating here is as good for your CV as it is for your stomach, with B-grade celebrities crowding the red-velvet-and-mirrors dining room. But the quality of the clientele doesn't affect the food, which is delectable Provençale cuisine. There's also the great new En Pluche next door, a grungier sister restaurant serving less posh nosh at cheaper prices.
☎ 679 71 76 ✉ Ruydaelstraat 54 ⏰ noon-2pm Mon-Fri, 6-11pm daily 🚋 3, 5, 12 ♿ fair

Mok Sam (3, D4) €
Surinamese & Chinese
If posh surrounds and dressed-up crowds are your thing, don't come here. But if you're after great Surinamese food and healthy, grease-free Chinese, this cheerful diner is perfect. A fantastic refuelling stop after the Albert Cuypmarkt, its huge *roti kip* portions (chicken curry, flaky roti with potatoes, egg and cabbage; €3.45) are tasty, and its *gado gado* unsurpassed.
☎ 671 13 96 ✉ Albert Cuypstraat 65 ⏰ 11am-10.30pm Mon-Sat, 1-10.30pm Sun 🚋 3, 5, 12, 16, 24 ♿ fair ♿ Ⓥ

Warung Mini (3, E3) €
Indonesian
Warung Mini's mix of Surinamese and Indonesian dishes keeps locals addicted. The staff are sweet and the food is as good as it smells.
☎ 662 55 15 ✉ Van Woustraat 19 ⏰ noon-10pm Tue-Sun 🚋 4 ♿ poor ♿ Ⓥ

Zen Japans Huis (3, C3) €€
Japanese
This classy Japanese restaurant, serving lunch and early dinners, gets especially busy with locals around 6pm each night. Its sushi and *don buri* are its specialities, though the tasty teriyaki set (€17) is an absolute wonder.
☎ 627 06 07 ✉ Frans Halsstraat 38 ⏰ noon-8pm Tue-Sat 🚋 4, 16, 24, 25 ♿ excellent Ⓥ

Highbrow Herring
The humble herring is ubiquitous in the Netherlands, served in snack bars, fish shops and restaurants alike. The little fish is so highly regarded that each May, Queen Beatrix is presented with the first catch of the year and regally opens the herring season.

RICHARD NEBESKY

Dutch-style fast food: the perennially popular herring with onion and gherkin

SOUTHERN CANAL BELT

Coffee & Jazz (3, E2) €€
Indonesian
A funky little joint with a loyal local following. Get cosy on a couch, order the spicy Boemboe Bali chicken curry and an extra-large mango juice and chill out to great jazz music.
☎ 624 58 51 ⊠ Utrechtsestraat 113 ⏱ 9.30am-8pm Tue-Fri, 10am-4pm Sat 🚇 4 ♿ fair 🚹 Ⓥ

Deshima Proeflokaal (3, C2) €
Vegetarian
This postage–stamp-sized macrobiotic restaurant is a herbivore's Valhalla. There's no denying its health value, as the wholesome glow of the clientele will attest. A changing daily menu features delicate yet hearty dishes such as miso soup and sautéed cabbage and paprika.
☎ 625 75 13 ⊠ Weteringschans 65 ⏱ noon-2pm Mon-Fri 🚇 6, 7, 10 🚹 Ⓥ poor

Dynasty (3, D1) €€€€
Asian
Decorated on a lavish *King & I* budget, this Southeast Asian eatery is resplendent with over-the-top murals and hundreds of rice-paper fans hanging from the ceiling. Dishes like 'salmon from the steam clouds' and 'thousand flower duck' taste as good as they sound (and are as pricey as they sound – mains €17 to €32).
☎ 626 84 00 ⊠ Reguliersdwarsstraat 30 ⏱ 5.30-11pm Wed-Mon 🚇 16, 24, 25 ♿ excellent 🚹 Ⓥ

La Rive (3, F3) €€€€
French
La Rive, at the ultra-posh Amstel InterContinental (p100), is the perfect big-night-out dinner destination. The superlative French cuisine has earned chef Edwin Kats his two Michelin stars and the formal dining room offers spanking views over the River Amstel. Booking is essential, and you should wear something swish unless you're rock 'n' roll enough to pull off casual dress.
☎ 622 60 60 ⊠ Professor Tulpplein 1 ⏱ lunch noon-2pm Mon-Fri, dinner 6.30-10.30pm daily 🚇 6, 7, 10 ♿ excellent

Le Pêcheur (3, D1) €€€
Seafood
Countless special nights have been spent salivating over the delectable seafood at Le Pêcheur, opened in 1981 by famed restaurateur Rien van Santen. The French-style seafood is perfectly prepared, but the true highlight is the terrace garden with its views of the Herengracht. Bookings are essential.
☎ 624 31 21 ⊠ Reguliersdwarsstraat 32 ⏱ noon-10.30pm Mon-Fri, 6-10.30pm Sat 🚇 16, 24, 25 ♿ fair Ⓥ

Get a healthy glow at Deshima Proeflokaal

Le Zinc...et Les Dames (3, D2) €€
French
Start with a drink at the Zinc bar downstairs in this romantic 16th-century canal house, then drag your date up to Les Dames for beautifully prepared French Mediterranean cuisine. The compact daily menu is accompanied by a long wine list. Booking is advisable.
☎ 622 90 44 ⊠ 1st fl, Prinsengracht 999
🕒 5.30-11pm Tue-Sat
🚊 16, 24, 25 ♿ fair

Moko (3, E2) €€€
International
In the basement of the Amstelkerk, where Napoleon used to tie up his horses, Moko is a classy purveyor of fusion food. The owners were planning a major makeover at the time of writing, but the venue's best asset – the wonderful outside terrace, a luxurious place to soak up some sun – will remain the same.
☎ 626 11 99 ⊠ Amstelveld 12 🕒 11am-1am (to 2am Fri & Sat) 🚊 4, 16, 24, 25 ♿ poor Ⓥ

Piet de Leeuw (3, D2) €€
Dutch
Amsterdam's top place for a hunk of meat, Piet de Leeuw has been improving

Amsterdammers' iron levels since the 1940s, and shows no signs of abating. Book ahead on weekends, and be extremely patient with the gruff staff when waiting for your mains – this cooked cow is worth the wait.
☎ 623 71 81
⊠ Noorderstraat 11
🕒 noon-11pm Mon-Fri, 5-11pm Sat & Sun 🚊 16, 24, 25 ♿ fair 🚻

Pygma Lion (3, D1) €€€
South African
This wonderful restaurant features a range of traditional South African dishes, ranging from ostrich kebabs to springbok steaks. It is also one of Amsterdam's most stylishly designed places to chow down. Go on, make a Boer of yourself.
☎ 420 70 22 ⊠ Nieuwe Spiegelstraat 5
🕒 11am-11pm Tue-Sat
🚊 1, 2, 5, 16, 24, 25
♿ excellent 🚻

Rose's Cantina (3, D1) €€
North & Latin American
¡Aye carumba! Any restaurant serving margaritas by the litre is sure to be as much fun as a barrel of monkeys. Expect megasize Tex-Mex meals, loud salsa music and icy drinks. The fajitas, tacos and *quesadillas* are too big for one, so make a friend and

share. Bookings are essential Thursday to Saturday.
☎ 625 97 97 ⊠ Reguliersdwarsstraat 38
🕒 5pm-1am (to 3am Fri & Sat) 🚊 1, 2, 5, 16, 24, 25 ♿ fair

Sluizer (3, E1) €€€
Seafood
This Amsterdam institution has a reputation for dependable seafood. Finicky fish lovers adore the traditional, expertly cooked dishes such as the fish of the day in béarnaise sauce. Book on Fridays and Saturdays and ask to be seated in the romantic enclosed garden terrace.
☎ 622 63 76 ⊠ Utrechtsestraat 43 🕒 noon-2.30pm Mon-Fri, 5-11pm daily 🚊 4 ♿ good
🚻 Ⓥ

Take Thai (3, E2) €€
Asian
If Tempo Doeloe (p74) is full or a bit much for your wallet to cope with, this snazzy designer-white restaurant is a good alternative. Choose from curries spiced according to your palate: 'soft', 'spicy' or 'killing'. The steamed fish is a speciality. Reservations are advisable.
☎ 622 05 77
⊠ Utrechtsestraat 87
🕒 6-10.30pm 🚊 4
♿ excellent 🚻 Ⓥ

Care for Some Food with that Smoke?

Smoking is still an entrenched habit in Amsterdam's dining spots. Larger places may have a nonsmoking section, but even the most self-righteous vegetarian establishments often have trouble banning smoking altogether.

In 2004, the City of Amsterdam tried to ban smoking in all bars, restaurants and enclosed public spaces. The uproar caused by cigarette-, beverage- and entertainment-industry lobbyists caused a government back flip, and it is now unclear when – if ever – the ban will be introduced.

Tempo Doeloe (3, E2) €€€
Indonesian
Ring the doorbell to this swish restaurant and you'll find the city's best Indonesian nosh. The classic dishes are much loved by diners with cash to splash on the ambience, which is enhanced by white linen and fine china. Reservations are essential.
☎ 625 67 18 ✉ Utrechtsestraat 75 🕙 6-11.30pm 🚊 4 ♿ good 🚇 Ⓥ

Wagamama (3, C2) €€
Japanese
London's hugely successful Japanese franchise has arrived and the locals love it. Ultra-healthy, reasonably priced (€8 to €13) noodle and rice dishes are served promptly at long benches in the slick-and-stark minimalist canteen. Perfect for a healthy lunch between museums, or a quick and simple dinner.
☎ 528 77 78 ✉ Max Euweplein 10 🕙 noon-11pm 🚊 1, 2, 5, 6, 7, 10 ♿ excellent 🚇 Ⓥ

Zuidlande (3, F2) €€€
French
The chef is a former Paul Bocuse protégé who left to start cooking his own creative French Mediterranean dishes in this beautifully furnished and lit restaurant. Relax back into one of their cosy wicker chairs and let yourself be cosseted by attentive staff and mesmerised by the dizzying desserts. Bookings are essential.
☎ 620 73 93 ✉ Utrechtsedwarsstraat 141 🕙 7-10.30pm Tue-Sat 🚊 4 ♿ poor

Sit & Stew
Culinary pleasure comes slowly in Amsterdam: many restaurants are used to groups of Dutch folk taking many long, gregarious hours to get through a meal. Consequently, many restaurants will take an age to bring your meal as their kitchens are only equipped to go at a slow rate.

WESTERN CANAL BELT

Café Morlang (2, A8) €€
Asian
Minimalist Morlang offers a quiet retreat from the shopping mayhem of nearby Leidsestraat. By day it's the place to flick through a fashion magazine while chomping on a healthy salad and taking in the gigantic portraits of staff and customers by local artist Peter Klashorst. At night, join well-groomed hipsters enjoying Asian-influenced dishes.
☎ 625 26 81 ✉ Keizersgracht 451 🕙 11am-1am Tue-Sun 🚊 1, 2, 5 ♿ poor

Café Walem (2, A8) €€
International
Next door to Morlang, this slick bar and restaurant was designed by famous Dutch architect Gerrit Rietveld, and has an 18-year history of pulling power with flashy trendsetters. In summer, you have two wonderful choices: eat by the canalside terrace or in the pretty garden courtyard (but be prepared to battle ruthlessly for the table you want).
☎ 625 35 44 ✉ Keizersgracht 449 🕙 10am-1am 🚊 1, 2, 5 ♿ poor

Chez Georges (2, B3) €€€
French
The western canal folk come to devour gourmet beef and eavesdrop (tables are very close) at this intimate upmarket restaurant. The French fare – Burgundian to be exact – is cooked with tender love by the Belgian owner. Best is the three-course set menu (€34).
☎ 626 33 32 ✉ Herenstraat 3 🕙 Mon & Tue, Thu-Sat 6-10.30pm 🚊 1, 2, 5, 13, 14, 17 ♿ poor

Quite the scene at diminutive Dimitri's

MARTIN MOOS

Christophe (5, C2)   €€€€
French
A Michelin star ensures Jean-Christophe Royer's swanky restaurant is always filled with sophisticated diners feasting on superlative Mediterranean-basin cuisine. They all bring a full wallet though: dishes such as roasted farm pigeon or terrine of young rabbit come with skyscraper-high price tags, with mains costing up to €40. Bookings are essential.
☎ 625 08 07
✉ Leliegracht 46
🕓 6.30-10.30pm Tue-Sat
🚋 13, 14, 17 ♿ fair

Christophe: all class

Dimitri's (2, A2)   €€
Salads & Sandwiches
Eating at Dimitri's is as much about positioning your brand as gaining nutritional benefit; this is a place to be seen breakfasting, as is clear from the procession of hip types nibbling on croissants each morning. But the laid-back design of this small café, combined with its tasty salads and sandwiches and the friendly staff, all make Being Seen fun.
☎ 627 93 93 ✉ Prinsenstraat 3 🕓 8am-10pm
🚋 1, 2, 5, 13, 17 ♿ poor
👶 Ⓥ

Foodism (2, A4)   €€
International
This funky little joint is run by a fun crew of chefs and waiters who are as happy working as they are sitting at your table having a chat. During the day they serve all-day breakfasts and good, honest sandwiches, while at night they dish out pasta, soups and salads.
☎ 427 51 03 ✉ Oude Leliestraat 8 🕓 11.30am-10pm Mon-Sat, 12.30-10pm Sun 🚋 1, 2, 5, 13, 14, 17 ♿ fair 👶 Ⓥ

Goodies (2, A7)   €€
Italian
Exquisitely simple and enticingly stylish, Goodies is a little pasta restaurant that also does simple daytime sandwiches. The cheery lighting, cosy open-plan setting and friendly staff make it popular with savvy locals right around the city.
☎ 625 61 22 ✉ Huidenstraat 9 🕓 9.30am-10.30pm Mon-Sat, 11am-4.30pm Sun 🚋 1, 2, 5 ♿ good 👶 Ⓥ

Hein (5, C4)   €
Breakfast & Lunch
Snappy suits and hip-to-the-groove types can't get enough of this ultramodern café and its home-away-from-home ethos. Walk through the industrial-style kitchen to get to the light-filled dining room, where you'll be served simple but delectable sandwiches and soups. On sunny days, the jousting for one of the three outdoor tables is ferocious.
☎ 623 10 48 ✉ Berenstraat 20 🕓 9am-6pm Wed-Mon 🚋 7, 10, 13, 14, 17 ♿ excellent 👶 Ⓥ

Lef (2, A7)   €
Sandwiches & Soup
This tiny sandwich-and-soup stop on a tiny street wedged between the Singel and Herengracht is a reliable spot to stop for lunch, with hearty, healthy fresh sandwiches (€3 to €5) and scrumptious apple pie and brownies, which the owners are quite proud of.
☎ 620 57 68 ✉ Wijde Heisteeg 1 🕓 9am-5.30pm (closed Tue) 🚋 1, 2, 5 ♿ excellent 👶 Ⓥ

Fine views, fine food at Metz & Co Café

Lust (5, C5) €
International
You might be disappointed to find out that *lust* is Dutch for appetite, but the healthy salads and pasta dishes at this new eatery won't disappoint. Look for the bright-green shopfront.
☎ 626 57 91
✉ Runstraat 13
🕙 10am-6pm (to 7pm Sat & Sun) 🚊 1, 2, 5, 13, 14, 17 ♿ excellent ♿ Ⓥ

Metz & Co Café (2, A8) €€
Breakfast & Lunch
The top-floor café of this swanky department store has sublime, panoramic views of the city centre. The food lives up to the views, too, with delicious sandwiches and salads, and great coffee.
☎ 520 70 36 ✉ Keizersgracht 455 🕙 11am-6pm Mon, 9.30am-6pm Tue-Sat (to 9pm Thu), Sun noon-5pm 🚊 1, 2, 5 ♿ excellent ♿

Pastini (5, C5) €€
Italian
Ensconced in the ludicrously picturesque spot where Leidsegracht and Keizersgracht meet is this wonderful Italian restaurant. No-one leaves without something nice to say about the staff, while the pasta is reliably good. Save room for the thrilling, filling desserts. Booking is advisable.
☎ 622 17 01 ✉ Leidsegracht 29 🕙 6-10pm 🚊 1, 2, 5, 7, 10 ♿ fair ♿

Singel 404 (2, A7) €
Sandwiches & Soup
On a beautiful spot by a bridge over the Singel, this simple eatery's canalside terrace fills up quickly on a sunny day, followed by the few tables inside. The smoked salmon salad is one of the city's freshest, and the apple crumble pie is a treat. If it's packed with fed-up shoppers waiting to be just-fed shoppers, pop round the corner to little Lef (p75).
☎ 428 01 54 ✉ Singel 404 🕙 noon-6pm 🚊 1, 2, 5, 13, 14, 17 ♿ excellent ♿ Ⓥ

Spanjer en van Twist (5, C2) €€
International
Spanjer en van Twist's canalside tables make it a popular destination on summer evenings. On grey days it's just as lovely inside with its high ceilings and stained glass. The affable staff serve affordable fare, including healthy sandwiches and pasta dishes, and uncomplicated international dishes such as fish pie and enchilada.
☎ 639 01 09 ✉ Leliegracht 60 🕙 10am-10pm (to 11pm Fri & Sat) 🚊 13, 14, 17 ♿ good ♿ Ⓥ

Sidewalk Snacks
In *Pulp Fiction*, well-travelled hit man Vincent Vega deadpans that ketchup is not the condiment of choice for french fries in Amsterdam. If you've tried a cone of *vlaamse frites* (french fries) smothered in mayonnaise or spicy peanut sauce, you won't be as aghast at this as Vincent's partner in crime, Jules. Dutch fries are made from whole potatoes rather than potato pulp, so you may be shocked at how much like potato these things actually taste (especially if you go easy on the mayo).

Other Amsterdam food-on-the-go options include fishy quick-fixes such as eel, normally served in a bun, and bite-sized salted herring served with chopped onion and gherkin.

Vincent was right: it is the little things that make all the difference.

't Buffet van Yvette & Odette (2, A6) €

International

You like Odette and Yvette and their beautiful light-filled café instantly upon reading their request not to use mobile phones in their restaurant 'unless absolutely necessary'. You're in love with them when you taste their delectable sandwiches, soup or quiches made with traditional or organic ingredients. The sticky toffee cake is out of this world.

☎ 423 60 34 ✉ Herengracht 309 ⏱ 8.30am-5.30pm Mon-Fri, 10am-5.30pm Sat, noon-5.30pm Sun 🚊 1, 2, 5 ♿ poor ♿ Ⓥ

Villa Zeezicht (2, B4) €

Breakfast & Lunch

Little Villa Zeezicht is so popular that sharing tables is practically *de rigueur*. Funky arts students, model mums and tourists all go for the same reason: the apple tart with cream. For €3 you get a mighty mountain of mushed apple, dusted with cinnamon and encased in warm flaky pastry. Lunches are great too.

☎ 626 74 33 ✉ Toren-steeg 7 ⏱ 7.30am-9pm 🚊 1, 2, 5, 13, 17 ♿ excellent ♿ Ⓥ

Zuid Zeeland (2, A8) €€€

Mediterranean

Romantic Zuid Zeeland is the dead-posh restaurant you'd expect to find in this ritzy neighbourhood – perfect for special dinners or celebrating the takeover you and your team just engineered. The elegant staff glide through the restaurant, with its terracotta walls and flower-filled vases, serving Mediterranean-inspired dishes.

☎ 624 31 54 ✉ Herengracht 413 ⏱ dinner 6-11pm, lunch noon-3pm Mon-Fri 🚊 1, 2, 5 ♿ poor Ⓥ

Pata Negra: tempting tapas keep the crowds coming

LATE-NIGHT EATS

Bojo (5, C6) €

Indonesian

Huge serves and reasonable prices have made Bojo an institution among late-night eaters, who head here post-nightclub for sizzling satays and filling plates of fried rice. Though the food ranges in quality from excellent to indifferent, service is always snappy.

☎ 622 74 34 ✉ Lange Leidsedwarsstraat 51 ⏱ 4pm-2am Mon-Thu (to 4am Fri & Sat), noon-2am Sun 🚊 1, 2, 5 ♿ good

Pata Negra (3, E2) €

Spanish

Fun and chaotic, Pata Negra serves tapas until midnight. Its alluringly tiled exterior is matched by its sparkling interior and moreish food (don't go past the garlic prawns and fish balls). It's quite a scene, with boisterous groups sharing jugs of sangria and tapas.

☎ 422 62 50 ✉ Utrecht-sestraat 124 ⏱ 2pm-1am (to 3am Fri & Sat) 🚊 4 ♿ good Ⓥ

Surinamese – Sure to Please

Food from Surinam, a former Dutch colony, is similar to Caribbean food, although over the centuries it has also picked up many influences from the food of Indonesia (another former Dutch colony). Hot and spicy chicken curries feature strongly, along with lamb, beef, potatoes, rice and delicious roti. Surinamese restaurants are usually small, specialising in takeaway food or quick sit-down meals.

Entertainment

Even the most jaded culture vulture will be impressed by Amsterdam's selection of canalside pubs, jazz venues, concert halls, rock concerts, hip-as-hell bars and clubs and cutting-edge experimental theatre, second to none in Europe. Cities like London and Paris might have more of everything, but they don't have Amsterdam's concentration of quality.

The city hosts festivals, cultural happenings and sporting events year round, but it really comes alive in summer. Catering to the tourist influx, theatres program English performances, and free, open-air entertainment takes place in parks, streets and on the canals.

Amsterdam's diverse ethnic mix and generous government arts funding has created a thriving arts scene with world-renowned ballet, philharmonic and opera companies. Cinemas screen all the latest blockbusters (in English) and art-house complexes show independent, cult and avant-garde films.

Amsterdam for Free

- Admire the view from the roof of NEMO (p27)
- Visit the Amsterdams Historisch Museum's free Civic Guard Gallery (p16)
- Join the in-line skaters outside the Nederlands Filmmuseum (p88; Friday 8pm) for a 15km skate through the city; watch for the toned rear end of the Buttman because he skates in a G-string
- Look around the antique stores and art galleries on Nieuwe Spiegelstraat and Spiegelgracht
- Climb the Zuiderkerk's tower (p34)

The city's music scene sizzles with local and international acts: everything from reggae and world-class jazz to chamber music. And, finally, those who come specifically to get stoned are well catered for by Amsterdam's hundreds of chilled-out coffeeshops.

For many entertainment venues listed here, you just need to turn up at the door and pay. Book ahead though for famous acts, opera and ballet performances. Contact the venues direct or book through the Uit Buro (p121) or the **Uitlijn** (☎ 0900-0191, per min €0.40; ☺ 9am-9pm).

For what's on information, try Uit Buro's free monthly paper, *Uitkrant*, available in theatres and bookshops, or Saturday's *Parool* newspaper.

Fashion-conscious fans (or victims?) of the House of Orange, celebrating Koninginnedag

Special Events
Mid-March *Blues Festival* Meervaart Theatre's thumping blues festival.

Mid-April to May *World Press Photo Exhibition* World's best press-photo exhibition, held in the Oude Kerk (p13).
Mid-April *National Museum Weekend* Free entry to many public museums.
30 April *Koninginnedag* Each year, Queen's Day (Koninginnedag) hits Amsterdam with the force of an atomic bomb (filled with beer, not uranium). More than a million revellers pour into Amsterdam to wish Queen Beatrix a happy birthday in their own special way – generally involving copious amounts of alcohol, loud music and good cheer. Those with kids in tow should head for Vondelpark, where kids' entertainment is the speciality. Gays and lesbians congregate at the Homomonument (p23) and Regulierswaardsstraat. Everyone else congregates, well, everywhere else.

2nd Saturday in May *National Windmill Day* Windmills unfurl their sails and open to the public.
Mid-May *Open Garden Days* View beautiful gardens hidden behind canal houses.
Late May–late August *Vondelpark Open Air Theatre* Live music, theatre, dance and kids' programs.

1st week of June *RAI Arts Fair* Massive contemporary-art exhibition.
June *Holland Festival* The country's biggest music, drama and dance extravaganza lasts all month and includes everything from highbrow world premieres to one-off fringe events.
June–August *Over het IJ Festival* Exciting performing-arts festival (dance, theatre, music) held at the former NDSM shipyards north of the IJ.

Mid-July *North Sea Jazz Festival* World's largest jazz festival (p89).

August *Amsterdam Pride* The city's premier gay and lesbian festival, held for three days starting the first weekend in August, and features the world's only gay float parade on water.
Last week of August *Uitmarkt* Free previews by local orchestras and theatre and dance troupes.

1st Saturday in September *Flower Parade* Spectacular procession of floats wends its way through the city and is illuminated by night.
2nd week in September *Jordaan Festival* Street festival with much merriment and entertainment.

Late October/early November *Crossing Border* Huge literary and music festival around Leidseplein attracting incredibly interesting and diverse guests; log onto www.crossingborder.nl.
Mid-November *Sinterklaas Parade* Christmas is launched when the Dutch Santa Claus arrives by steamboat and distributes sweets to kids.
3rd week in November *Cannabis Cup* Marijuana festival with the cup going to the best grass and other awards given for the biggest spliff.

5 December *Sinterklaas* Gift-giving, in honour of St Nicholas.

BARS & CAFÉS

With an average yearly consumption of 336 glasses of beer per person, the Dutch do a lot of drinking. Of course, this makes for some very sociable types, and Amsterdam's bars and cafés are wonderful places to mix with locals. This is a town to let go of social conventions and gabber with anyone you can be bothered with.

Most bars and cafés serve food (from simple toasted sandwiches to fancy French cuisine) and some have outdoor seating (terraces) that are covered and heated in winter.

CENTRUM: OLD SIDE

Blincker (2, C6)
The high ceiling and attractive open mezzanine aren't the only things making Blincker a great theatre café. At the rear of the Frascati Theatre (p91), Blincker is packed most nights with an unpretentious, young crowd, chatting away or eating a bowl of their excellent soup. ☎ 627 19 38 🖥 www.nestheaters.nl ✉ Sint Barberenstraat 7-9 🕐 4pm-1am (to 3pm Fri & Sat) 🚊 4, 9, 16, 24, 25 ♿ good

De Buurvrouw (2, C6)
A model of *de Buurvrouw* (the woman neighbour) watches with suspicious eyes from above the door. She's right to be wary, because if you end up at this tucked-away bar-of-last-resort, it's likely you've been drinking for several hours. Live bands perform some weeknights, and DJs play a good range of alternative pop and rock on weekends. ☎ 625 96 54 ✉ Sint Pieterspoortsteeg 29 🕐 9pm-3am (to 4am Fri & Sat) 🚊 4, 9, 16, 24, 25 ♿ excellent

De Kroon (3, E1)
Escape Rembrandtplein's tourist schlock at this oh-so-glam grand café. De Kroon's colonial design comes with a biological bent (cabinets with pinned butterflies and ancient microscopes) and a beautiful covered balcony terrace. It's in the same building as radio and TV stations, so there's a preponderance of loud talkers; the café's sheer size should be enough to avoid them. ☎ 625 20 11 ✉ 1st fl, Rembrandtplein 17 🕐 noon-1am (to 3am Fri & Sat) 🚊 4, 9, 14 ♿ poor

---

A Bar by Any Other Name Would Smell as Sweet

Brown cafés, grand cafés, beer cafés... Confused? All you need to remember is that 'café' in this town means a place for drinking booze.

A true brown café has been in business for up to 400 years, is stained by cigarette smoke (recent aspirants simply slap on brown paint), has sand on the wooden floor, and sometimes Persian rugs on the tables to soak up spills.

Spacious and comfortable, grand cafés are all the rage; any pub that installs a few solid tables and comfy chairs will call itself a grand café.

Beer cafés are drinking dens, pure and simple. This is the place to do your best power drinking.

Eetcafes take their food seriously, and their food can be very good indeed.

Bars attached to a theatre are known as theatre cafés and are wonderful for a pre- or post-theatre drink amid flocks of flamboyant dramatists and drama queens. They usually do great food too.

The last few years have seen an explosion of ultra-hip lounge bars – some ultra-modern, others retro-loungey or shabby-chic.

The primary function of coffeeshops (p94), is to sell you as much dope as you can burn in one sitting. They also sell coffee and sometimes alcohol. Don't go to a *koffee-huis* expecting reefer madness – these are genuine places for a coffee and a sandwich.

Two Fingers to You

Dutch beer is served cold and with a head of two fingers of froth. Word is that this traps the flavour, and can also reveal whether the beer has been watered down – if it has, the head will sink quickly, while unwatered beer will retain its head for up to five minutes. First-timers often think they're being had, but barkeepers usually meet requests of 'no head please' with a steely response.

Lokaal 't Loosje (2, E5)

One of the area's oldest brown cafés, Lokaal 't Loosje started life as a tram shelter. It's still a scruffy-round-the-edges kind of place, though in a deeply groovy Dutch way. It's a great place for late-night drinking or a morning coffee, and attracts a lively student crowd. Don't be too precious about the service, though – the gruff demeanour is part of the package.
☎ 627 26 35 ✉ Nieuw-markt 32-34 ⏱ 9.30am-1am (to 3am Fri & Sat) Ⓜ Nieuwmarkt ♿ good

CENTRUM: NEW SIDE
Bep (2, B5)

Bep is a wonderfully laid-back lounge bar. Things start heating up after 8pm when gaggles of experimental film-makers, photographers and other wearers of sepia-tinted sunglasses arrive. Diep next door is just as hep to the groove, and keeps the same hours, so take your pick.
☎ 626 56 49 ✉ Nieu-wezijds Voorburgwal 260 ⏱ 4.30pm-1am Mon-Thu, to 3am Fri, 11am-3am Sat, 11am-1am Sun 🚊 1, 2, 5, 13, 17 ♿ excellent

Cafe het Schuim (2, B5)

Schuim translates as 'foam', as in the foam on your beer, and 'scum', as in the coke dealers circulating this grungy bar. A mind-boggling mix of humanity gathers here to drink, laugh, dance: students, middle-aged accountants, older creative types, you name it. All brought together by great music. And drugs.
☎ 638 93 57 ✉ Spui-straat 189 ⏱ 11am-1am Mon-Thu, to 3am Fri & Sat, 1pm-1am Sun 🚊 1, 2, 5, 13, 14, 17 ♿ excellent

Hoppe (2, A7)

This constantly packed brown café has been setting 'em up for thirsty drinkers for over 300 years. Some serious drinking gets done here: Hoppe has the city's highest beer turnover (a liver-crunching 300,000L a year). With its beer barrels and recycled church pews for seats, the dark bar has a cosy ambience.
☎ 420 44 20 ✉ Spui 18 ⏱ 8am-1am Mon-Thu, to 2am Fri & Sat 🚊 1, 2, 5 ♿ excellent

Luxembourg (2, A7)

Get glamorous on a grand scale at Luxembourg. Take a seat at the library-style reading table or on the glassed-in terrace overlooking the Spui, order the Royale snack platter and flutter your eyelashes at all the tanned Euro princes and princesses. If the snooty staff aren't rude to you, you must've been mistaken for someone more famous.
☎ 620 62 64 ✉ Spui 22-24 ⏱ 9am-1am (to 2am Fri & Sat) 🚊 1, 2, 5 ♿ good

Cutting loose at the Lokaal 't Loosje

MARTIN MOOS

JORDAAN

Cafe Thijssen (2, A1)

All variety of cheery Jordaan locals booze on at this laid-back bar, from unstudious students to pinstriped bankers. And they come in droves, the bar regularly packed to the rafters with a crowd ranging in age from 25-35. They do excellent light meals and soups too. ☎ 623 89 94 ✉ Brouwersgracht 107 ⏲ 8am-1am (to 3am Fri & Sat) ♿ 13, 17 ♿ good

Finch (2, A1)

On one of Jordaan's prettiest squares, Finch and its retro décor draws the hippest locals and arty types. This lounge bar is a great place to eat after visiting the market (or, on Monday mornings, before the market). Proust next door is equally good. ☎ 626 24 61 ✉ Noordermarkt 5 ⏲ 8am-1am Mon, 11am-1am Tue-Sun (to 3am Fri & Sat) ♿ 1, 2, 5, 13, 17 ♿ excellent

> ## Cin-Cin to Dutch Gin
>
> *Genever* (Dutch gin) is made from juniper berries and drunk chilled from thimble-size glasses or on the rocks. Most people prefer smooth *jonge* (young) *genever*; *oude* (old) *genever* has a strong juniper flavour and is an acquired taste. A common combination, called a *kopstoot* (head butt), is a glass of *genever* with a beer chaser. More than a few *kopstoot* will definitely lead to a *hoofdpijn* (headache). You can try dozens of *genevers* and liqueurs at *proeflokaalen* (tasting houses), which used to be attached to distilleries – a hangover from the 17th century when scores operated around town.

Het Papeneiland (2, A1)

With its Delft blue tiles, huge ceramic beer jugs and central stove, Het Papeneiland is a 17th-century gem. The name, Papists' Island, goes back to the Reformation when there was a secret tunnel running from this brown café to a clandestine Catholic church across the canal. ☎ 624 19 89 ✉ Prinsengracht 2 ⏲ 10am-1am Mon-Sat (to 2am Fri & Sat), noon-1am Sun ♿ 1, 2, 3, 5, 13, 17 ♿ excellent

't Smalle (5, C2)

Opened in 1786 as a gin distillery and tasting house, this utterly charming brown café has such a stunning, picturesque canalside terrace it's a wonder anyone ever ventures inside. Poke your head in, if only to note the antique porcelain beer pumps and impressive leadlighting. ☎ 623 96 17 ✉ Egelantiersgracht 12 ⏲ 10am-1am ♿ 10, 13, 14, 17 ♿ good

All bright and chirpy at Finch

SOUTHERN CANAL BELT

Cafe Americain (5, C6)

Opened in 1902, Cafe Americain is the oldest and most stylish grand café in Amsterdam. Its Art Deco interior, vaulted roof and stained-glass windows are a must-see.

☎ 556 32 32
✉ Leidsekade 97
🕐 7am-10pm 🚊 1, 2, 5, 6, 7, 10 ♿ excellent

De Balie (3, B2)

Politics and beer are the main things on the menu at de Balie, which is attached to a cultural centre of the same name. It's the place to meet before and after one of the documentary screenings, political debates or lectures (many in English) held at the centre. In winter they have DJs on weekend nights playing mellow tunes.

☎ 553 51 00 🖥 www .balie.nl in Dutch
✉ Kleine Gartmanplantsoen 10 🕐 1pm-1am (to 3am Fri & Sat) 🚊 1, 2, 5, 6, 7, 10 ♿ poor

Kamer 401 (5, B6)

The clients are mostly aspirational *Sex and the City* types, but this yuppie paradise is perfect for a quiet pre-theatre, or raucous post-theatre, drink. Kamer's lounge bar design is stylish, especially the luxuriant lighting that makes everyone look like a movie star.

☎ 422 44 53
✉ Marnixstraat 401
🕐 4pm-1am (to 3am Fri & Sat) 🚊 1, 2, 5, 6, 7, 10 ♿ poor

Lux (5, B6)

You'd think this split-level lounge bar was too slick to draw the vaguely alternative crowd it does. DJs play some good tunes, making it one of the area's most happening places when it's late. Next door is Weber, which also draws a crowd most nights.

☎ 422 14 12 ✉ Marnixstraat 403 🕐 8pm-3am (to 4am Fri & Sat) 🚊 1, 2, 5, 6, 7, 10 ♿ poor

De Smoeshaan (5, B6)

Smoes means people whispering the latest gossip, *haan* means cock (as in chicken). So, expect lots of whispering chickens at Theater Bellevue's café. Grab the big round table by the stairs in this small, dark temple of intellectualism and start gabbing.

☎ 625 03 68 ✉ Leidsekade 90 🕐 11am-1am (to 2am Fri & Sat) 🚊 1, 2, 5, 6, 7, 10 ♿ poor

Style on a grand scale at grand Cafe Americain

WESTERN CANAL BELT

Cafe de Pels (5, C5)

A cartoon of a satisfied shaggy dog is the mascot of this local brown café, and it sums the place up well: scruffy, relaxed and cheeky. It's a lovely place to get sloshed, with students, professionals and pointy-headed intellectuals all drinking together in solidarity.

☎ 622 90 37 ✉ Huidenstraat 25 🕙 10am-1am (to 2am Fri & Sat) 🚊 1, 2, 5 ♿ Excellent

Cafe van Zuylen (2, B4)

Packed nightly with a peculiar mix of slick suits and dishevelled students, polished Cafe van Zuylen has a jovial atmosphere of good cheer and flowing beer. It also does a tasty line in croissants and pastries in the morning and soups at lunch, served on the picturesque bridge over the Singel.

Even the bikes are hip at Wolvenstraat 23

☎ 639 10 55 ✉ Torensteeg 4 🕙 10am-1am (to 3am Fri & Sat) 🚊 1, 2, 5, 13, 17 ♿ good

De Vergulde Gaper (2, A2)

A funky former pharmacy decorated with old chemists' bottles and vintage posters. Arrive in the afternoon, order a flaky filled croissant and get cosy on the couch. Otherwise get busy on the terrace with all those shiny, happy people meeting for an after-work drink.

Swish brown café, Van Puffelen

☎ 624 89 75 ✉ Prinsenstraat 30 🕙 10am-1am (to 3am Fri & Sat) 🚊 13, 14, 17 ♿ fair

Van Puffelen (5, C4)

Popular with the cashed-up professional crowd, Van Puffelen is one of Amsterdam's largest and busiest brown cafés. Divided into cosy nooks and romantic alcoves, its two huge rooms are quite intimate, though. The lunchtime tapas are delicious.

☎ 624 62 70 ✉ Prinsengracht 377 🕙 3pm-1am Mon-Thu, noon-2am Fri & Sat, to 1am Sun 🚊 13, 14, 17 ♿ good

Wolvenstraat 23 (5, C4)

A beguilingly hip little bar where beautiful young people come to quaff wine and pout seductively. It does healthy breakfasts, scrumptious snacks, and reliable Chinese at night. It's a good choice for a subdued drink, as the weekend crowds will attest. The owners also run Finch (p82).

☎ 320 08 43 ✉ Wolvenstraat 23 🕙 8am-1am (to 2am Fri & Sat) 🚊 1, 2, 5 ♿ good

DE PIJP
Chocolate (3, D4)
In a great spot in De Pijp, this funky little bar thinks it's a bit too-cool-for-school. However, its terrace more than makes up for the attitude. And its Monday night art-house film screenings (€12 including dinner) are a winner.

☎ 675 76 72 ✉ 1e van der Helststraat 62a ⏱ Sun-Thu 10am-1am, Fri & Sat to 3am 🚃 3, 16, 24, 25 ♿ excellent

De Engel (3, E4)
No visit to the Albert Cuypmarkt (p51) is complete without a drink at De Engel, a grand café in an old church with a soaring vaulted ceiling. The eclectic interior is a wonder: 1920s lamps from an Antwerp casino, a 1930s Paris nightclub bar, upstairs lighting from New York. There's live jazz and classical music here on weekends.

☎ 675 05 44 ✉ Albert Cuypstraat 182 ⏱ 11am-10pm (to 1am Fri & Sat) 🚃 16, 24, 25 ♿ poor

Kingfisher (3, D4)
Kingfisher's understated cool combined with its light and airy interior and intelligent crowd make it unbeatable. The tables are roomy, the design hip without pretence and the menu cheap but good.

☎ 671 23 95 ✉ Ferdinand Bolstraat 24 ⏱ 11am-1am Mon-Sat (to 3am Fri & Sat) 🚃 16, 24, 25 ♿ excellent

JODENBUURT, PLANTAGE & THE WATERFRONT
Bierbrouwerij 't IJ (4, E6)
You'd expect tourists seeking the authentic Dutch Experience™ to flock to this brewery, which lies under the shadow of the De Gooyer windmill (p31). But on sunny evenings, it's mostly locals relaxing outside in its shadow, and drinking the wonderful beers.

☎ 622 83 25 ✉ Funenkade 7 ⏱ 3-7.45pm Wed-Sun 🚃 9, 14 ♿ good

De IJsbreker (1, D4)
De IJsbreker music centre boasts a grand café with one of Amsterdam's top terraces; as if that weren't enough, the cosy Art Deco café is also perfect for a deep and meaningful chat in winter. Order a beer and toasted sandwich and mix it with the country's leading experimental musicians. Service can be incredibly slow – it's part of the bohemian charm.

☎ 668 18 05 🖳 www.ysbreker.nl ✉ Weesperzijde 23 ⏱ 10am-1am (to 2am Fri & Sat) 🚃 3 ♿ poor

Odessa (1, F3)
Odessa rocks. Literally. Opposite KNSM Eiland, this groovy boat, with outdoor eating decks and a 1970s-themed 'plush-porno' basement disco, is the sort of place where Hugh Hefner would hold a debauched pyjama party. Make your own mischief here while enjoying the terrific meaty menu.

☎ 419 30 10 ✉ Veemkade 259 ⏱ 6pm-1am Mon, 11am-1am Tue-Sun 🚃 28, 32, 59 ♿ poor

De Sluyswacht (2, E6)
No, you're not drunk: this brown café is leaning heavily. It's been here since 1695 though, so the foundations seem to be holding. The terrace surrounding this former lock-keeper's house is just the place on summer afternoons, especially out back by the canal, while in winter the bar's a cosy place.

☎ 330 94 63 ✉ Jodenbreestraat 1 ⏱ 11.30am-1am Mon-Thu, to 3am Fri & Sat, Sun to 7pm 🚃 9, 14 ♿ poor

De IJsbreker: a ground-breaking music centre and cosy café

MARTIN MOOS

CLUBS

Thursday and Saturday are the busiest nights for clubbing in Amsterdam, with Friday and Sunday close behind. Not much happens before 11pm and all venues close at 5am. Dress standards are pretty casual so you may feel out of place dressed up in designer duds.

Bitterzoet (2, C3)

Bittersweet's entry policy? Wearers of suits and dress shoes aren't welcome. The lounge interior hosts live music some nights, and there's a constantly changing schedule of hip-hop, world music and jazz. ☎ 521 30 01 🖳 www .bitterzoet.com in Dutch ✉ Spuistraat 2 € €5-12 🕑 8pm-3am (to 4am Fri & Sat) 🚊 1, 2, 5,13, 17 ♿ good

Cafe Meander (2, B7)

Locals consider a visit to Meander even more embarrassing than dancing the night away at nearby student haunt Dansen Bij Jansen (Handboogstraat 11, which now requires university ID to get into). But Meander is a fun, cheery place, packed with 20-somethings after cheap beer and the equally cheap music – sexed-up MTV current chart toppers and classic disco tunes. ☎ 625 84 30 ✉ Voetboogstraat 5 € €3-8 🕑 11pm-3am Tue-Thu, to 4am Fri & Sat 🚊 1, 2, 4, 5, 9, 16, 24, 25 ♿ good

Eleven (4, A3)

Housed in Amsterdam's hottest new bar and restaurant, high above the city on the 11th floor of the old post office building (with the Stedelijk Museum CS downstairs, p15), Eleven (or Club Eleven at night) is the place to be seen for the moment. Its house and garage soundtrack and spectacular skyline views make for a sure-fire formula to dance the night away. ☎ 573 29 11 ✉ Oosterdokskade 5 € €5-14 🕑 8pm-3am Tue-Sat 🚌 28, 32 ♿ excellent

Jimmy Woo's (5, C6)

All Amsterdam knows how hard it is to get into Jimmy Woo's. With space for 500-plus beautiful people, this sleek club just off Leidseplein is not small. But the freezing crowds out front most nights will give an idea of its popularity. It plays garage and hip-hop most nights. ☎ 626 31 50 ✉ Korte Leidsedwarsstraat 18 € €8 🕑 8pm-3am Wed & Thu, to 4am Fri & Sat 🚊 1, 2, 5, 6, 7, 10 ♿ fair

Don't be fooled: it might look like an old energy station but, inside, Panama is pure style

Melkweg (5, C6)

Housed in a former dairy, the Melkweg (Milky Way) is Amsterdam's funkiest multifunctional entertainment venue; there's a cinema, art gallery, café, nightclub and concert hall. The club has a changing program of nights, but there's always something fun coming up. Music is everything from jazz trance to Caribbean and African dance parties.
☎ 531 81 81 ⌨ www .melkweg.nl ✉ Lijn-baansgracht 234a € free–€15 ☼ hours vary; check website 🚊 1, 2, 5, 6, 7, 10 ♿ excellent

Panama (1, E3)

Housed inside the old harbour energy station, this ultra-impressive deluxe club and bar is now powered by pricey cocktails and stylish 30-somethings drinking with merry abandonment. It's been here for a few years now, but will the glamorous crowds will arrive en masse when the Lloyd Hotel opens (p100).
☎ 311 86 87 ⌨ www .panama.nl ✉ Oostelijke Handelskade 4 € €5-12 ☼ 8pm-3am Wed & Thu, to 4am Fri & Sat 🚌 32, 39

Paradiso (3, C2)

Amsterdam's premier live-music venue becomes a club after the band's done, usually around midnight. Expect hip-hop and hard house on Friday and Saturday nights. The young crowd is decked out in everything from street wear to designer labels, and Saturday's Paradiso is crammed-to-the-rafters popular.

☎ 626 45 21 ⌨ www .paradiso.nl ✉ Weter-ingschans 6 € €8-12 ☼ Fri-Sun 11.30pm-4am 🚊 6, 7, 10 ♿ poor

Winston International (2, D4)

This small venue plays everything: hip-hop and '80s glam to open-mic poetry readings. It even stretches to classic disco some nights. It's a fascinating and often wild place to party, because you never know what to expect. Ask at the hotel attached to the club during the day if you're curious.
☎ 623 13 80 ⌨ www .winston.nl ✉ War-moesstraat 129 € €5-10 ☼ 10pm-3am (to 4am Fri & Sat) 🚊 4, 9, 16, 24, 25 ♿ good

RICHARD NEBESKY

Pump it up at Paradiso

CINEMAS

Amsterdam's small number of cinemas is compensated for by the good choice of films, including many art-house movies. With the exception of children's flicks, films are screened in their original language with Dutch subtitles (because, according to one usher, 'Dubbing is *sooo* German!') Dutch films have 'Nederlands Gesproken' after the title.

Bellevue Cinerama & The Calypso (5, B6)

These two adjacent Pathe cinemas share the same box office. Both show mainstream blockbusters, but the Cinerama's basement cinema also screens recent and classic art-house films.
☎ 0900-14 58 (per min €0.40) 💻 www.pathe.nl ✉ Marnixstraat 400 € €6-9 ⏱ 11am-midnight 🚊 7, 10 ♿ excellent

Kriterion (1, E4)

Opposite the University of Amsterdam and housed in a much-loved Amsterdam School building, the Kriterion shows a lively mix of cult, classic and kids' flicks, with occasional sneak previews of upcoming films. Go early and drink with spotty, politically active types in the down-at-heel bar.

Kriterion for cult, classic or kids' flicks

☎ 623 17 08 💻 www.kriterion.nl in Dutch ✉ Roetersstraat 170 € €7.50/6 ⏱ 10am-late (bar 11am-1am Mon-Fri, 1pm-1am Sat & Sun) 🚊 6, 7, 10 ♿ good

Melkweg (5, C6)

Melkweg (see also p87) has a creative little cinema running a selection of films ranging from art-house and cult to the better Hollywood productions.
☎ 531 81 81 ✉ Lijnbaansgracht 234a € €6/4 🚊 1, 2, 5, 6, 7, 10 ♿ excellent

The Movies (1, C2)

Four screens here exhibit a mixed bag of the better mainstream films, kitsch cult, avant-garde Euro flicks and rarely screened gems. A meal in the Wild Kitchen, the gorgeous Art Deco restaurant attached to the cinema, is a perfect prelude to an intermission-free film.
☎ 638 60 16 💻 www.themovies.nl ✉ Haarlemmerdijk 161 € adult/student/child €8/7/6.50 ⏱ 1.30pm-midnight 🚊 1, 2, 3, 5, 13, 17 ♿ good

Nederlands Filmmuseum (3, A2)

There's not much in the way of museum, but plenty in the way of film at this beautiful Vondelpark

Catch a creepy classic at Nederlands Filmmuseum

pavilion. The museum owns more than 40,000 films and regularly screens everything from silent classics to contemporary Iranian art-house. In summer after dark on Fridays, films are shown outdoors on the beautiful terrace; with only 250 seats, you'll need to come early.
☎ 589 14 00 💻 www.filmmuseum.nl ✉ Vondelpark 3 ⏱ €6.25/3.75 daytime sessions, €11 evenings, €2.50 outdoor screenings 🚊 1, 3, 5, 6, 12 ♿ good

Tuschinskitheater (2, C8)

One of Europe's most beautiful cinemas, this Art Deco monument is worth a visit for its interior alone (p34). The main cinema offers a steady stream of blockbusters, while its Art-House offers slightly quirkier fare.
☎ 626 26 33 💻 www.pathe.nl ✉ Reguliersbreestraat 26 € €8-10 ⏱ noon-10pm 🚊 4, 9, 14 ♿ poor

ROCK, JAZZ & BLUES

Its relaxed vibe (and the drugs) makes Amsterdam a popular destination for rock stars. Naturally for such an intellectual city, jazz is also big. The blues scene is smaller but lively.

Information and tickets are available at the Uit Buro (p121) or at the venues direct, but for large pop concerts you can also ring the **Postbank ticket service** (☎ 0900-30 01 25; €0.40 per min).

Bamboo Bar – always fun, but especially after the clock strikes one

Akhnaton (2, C3)
This self-described 'centre for world culture' is known for its African dance and salsa parties, as well as occasional Middle Eastern and world music nights.
☎ 624 33 96 ✉ Nieuwezijds Kolk 25-27
€ €5-7 ☾ 11pm-5am Fri & Sat 🚊 1, 2, 5, 13, 17 ♿ poor

Alto Jazz Cafe (3, C2)
A renowned live venue, Alto is a great place to hear clas-sic and contemporary jazz compositions. It's easy to find: just listen for the jumping jazz and blistering blues tunes spilling out of this small, smoky brown café.
☎ 626 32 49 ✉ Korte Leidsedwarsstraat 115
€ free ☾ 9pm-3am (to 4am Fri & Sat) 🚊 1, 2, 5, 6, 7, 10 ♿ good

ArenA Stadium (1, E6)
The ultimate stadium venue for the blockbuster touring shows. Join 52,000 other fans trying to work out which little dot in the distance is Britney, Madonna or Robbie. It's also home to the Ajax football team.
☎ 311 13 33 🖥 www.amsterdamarena.nl ✉ Arena Boulevard 1, Bijlmer € prices vary ☾ box office 9am-6pm Ⓜ 54 (in the direction of Gein) ♿ excellent

Bamboo Bar (5, C6)
Squish into this tiny bar to hear live jazz, blues, pop and salsa. The vibes are friendly and the drinks well priced, but the room gets megasmoky.
☎ 624 39 93 ✉ Lange Leidsedwarsstraat 64
€ free ☾ 8pm-3am (to 4am Fri & Sat) 🚊 1, 2, 5, 6, 7, 10 ♿ poor

Hot Jazz
The North Sea Jazz Festival, the world's largest jazz festival, is held in The Hague each July and many international greats also gig around Amsterdam venues before and afterwards. For information, contact the VVV or the Amsterdam Uit Buro (p121).

Latin American & World Music

Amsterdam is the European centre for music from the most distant parts of the world. Here's where to hear marvellous mambo, sexy salsa or riotous rai music.

Canecão (3, C2; ☎ 626 15 00; Lange Leidsedwarsstraat 70) plays live samba, salsa and Brazilian music nightly. The Tropenmuseum's **Soeterijntheater** (1, E4; ☎ 568 85 0 0; Linnaeusstraat 2), celebrates non-Western culture with regular South American, Indian and African music and dance performances.

Bimhuis (2, F6)

Amsterdam's leading jazz venue has been hosting performances of big-name international and local acts in its excellent auditorium for over 25 years. The Bimhuis and the IJsbreker (p85) have for several years promised to move to a swanky new Docklands location; construction of their new building is underway and expected to finish in early 2005. Ring ahead.
☎ 623 13 61 ⌨ www .bimhuis.nl ✉ Oudeschans 73-77 € €8-16 ☺ 10.30pm-2am Mon-Wed, 9pm-2am Thu-Sat ⊞ 4, 9, 14 ⅋ poor

Maloe Melo (5, B4)

Home to the city's thriving blues scene, this venue features a full roster of local and international acts. When the live roots and blues get too much, mooch off to Korsakoff (☎ 625 78 54, Lijnbaansgracht 161), the live-rock venue next door.
☎ 420 45 92 ✉ Lijnbaansgracht 163 € free ☺ 9pm-3am (to 4am Fri-Sun) ⊞ 6, 7, 10 ⅋ fair

Melkweg (5, C6)

Melkweg (p87) has a live-music program that includes top international acts and local talent playing everything from didgeridoo to double bass.
☎ 624 17 77 ⌨ www .melkweg.nl ✉ Lijnbaansgracht 234 € free or €2 ☺ 7.30pm-4am Sun & Tue-Thu, to 5am Fri & Sat ⅋ excellent

Paradiso (3, C2)

In the '60s, this neo-Gothic church was the hub of all things flower power; today it's the number-one venue for big acts seeking some street cred. The Rolling Stones recorded a live album here years ago, and influential names such as Prince and Public Enemy have done time beneath its towering ceiling and high balconies.
☎ 626 45 21 ⌨ www .paradiso.nl ✉ Weteringschans 6 € €5-15 ☺ 8.30pm-4am ⊞ 6, 7, 10 ⅋ good

Westergasfabriek (1, C2)

This former gas factory hosts the odd rock concert in its old, round gas-holder, as well as the wildly popular annual Drum Rhythm Festival. Major development work to remove asbestos and decontaminate soil has been ongoing since 2002, and still means it's open sporadically. Ring ahead.
☎ 621 12 11 or 488 77 78 (Uit Buro) ✉ Haarlemmerweg 8-10 € varies ☺ varies ⊞ 10 ⅋ good

Never heard a Dutch didgeridoo? Make haste for Melkweg

THEATRE & COMEDY

Amsterdam's fertile cultural landscape has nurtured a huge variety of theatres, presenting everything from radical, experimental productions to Broadway-style musicals. Apart from big touring shows, performances are mainly in Dutch, though in summer some companies perform in English.

Boom Chicago (5, C6)

This English-language improv troupe has been entertaining locals and tourists for years. Their hilarious shows are fast paced and fraught with double entendres.
☎ 423 01 01 🖥 www.boomchicago.nl
✉ Leidseplein 12
€ €10-17.50
🕑 11.30am-8.30pm (to 11pm Fri & Sat) 🚊 1, 2, 5, 6, 7, 10 ♿ excellent

Felix Meritis (5, C4)

Born the same year as the French Revolution and once the city's main cultural centre, Felix Meritis (Latin for 'happy through merit') has staged some hot acts in its time, including Brahms and Mozart. Today the space is used by experimental and emerging European theatre, music and dance troupes.
☎ 626 23 21 🖥 www.felixmeritis.nl ✉ Keizersgracht 324 € €5-25
🕑 box office 10am-5pm Mon-Sat 🚊 1, 2, 5, 13, 14, 17 ♿ excellent

Frascati (2, C6)

Young Dutch directors, choreographers and producers strut their stuff at this experimental theatre venue. There are lots of multicultural dance and music performances, as well as monthly hip-hop, rap and break-dancing nights. Performances are often in Dutch.

Bank on big laughs at Boom Chicago

☎ 626 68 66 (day), 623 57 23 (evening)
🖥 www.nestheaters.nl
✉ Nes 63 € €7-14
🕑 1-6pm Mon-Sat
🚊 4, 9, 16, 24, 25 ♿ fair

Koninklijk Theater Carré (3, F1)

Built in 1887, Koninklijk Theater Carré is the largest theatre in town (1700 seats) hosting everything from three-ringed circuses and musicals to Van Morrison. You'll also find the occasional bout of opera, operetta and ballet.
☎ 622 52 25 🖥 www.theatercarre.nl ✉ Amstel 115-125 € €10-47.50
🕑 box office 10am-7pm Mon-Sat, 1-7pm Sun 🚊 4, 6, 7, 10 ♿ excellent

Stadsschouwburg (5, C6)

This neo-Renaissance edifice, built in 1894, is the city's most beautiful theatre. It hosts large-scale productions, operas, operettas and, in summer, English-language performances. Try

the attached Cafe Cox for a pre-theatre drink or post-performance debrief.
☎ 624 23 11 ✉ Leidseplein 26 € prices vary
🕑 box office 10am-8pm Mon-Sat, to 6.30pm Sun
🚊 1, 2, 5, 6, 7, 10
♿ excellent

Theater Bellevue & Nieuwe de la Mar Theater (5, B6)

These two theatre groups merged in the 1980s, but both kept their own specialities. Bellevue mostly does popular theatre, with occasional plays in English, while Nieuwe de la Mar does experimental dance, Dutch cabaret and the odd mime performance (God bless 'em).
☎ 530 53 01 (Bellevue), 530 53 02 (Nieuwe de la Mar) 🖥 www.theaterbellevue.nl in Dutch
✉ Leidsekade 90 (Bellevue), Marnixstraat 404 (Nieuwe de la Mar)
€ €7-16 🕑 box office 11am-6pm 🚊 1, 2, 5, 6, 7, 10 ♿ excellent

CLASSICAL MUSIC, OPERA & DANCE

The Dutch love classical music and arts with an at-times obsessive passion. Ticket prices are reasonable, especially in comparison to countries such as Germany or Austria, although tickets can be hard to get to big performances. For cut-price tickets on the day try the **AUB** (☎ 0900-0191; Leidseplein) or go to www.uitlijn.nl (in Dutch).

Beurs van Berlage (2, D4)
The city's former commodities exchange now houses two small concert halls worth visiting for their stunning Art Nouveau interiors, comfortable seats and state-of-the-art acoustics. The Beurs is home to the Netherlands Philharmonic and the Netherlands Orchestra.
☎ 621 12 11 🖥 www .beursvanberlage.nl ✉ **Damrak 243** € €7-20 ☟ **buy tickets from Stadsschouwburg box office (Leidseplein 26), 10am-8pm Mon-Sat, to 6.30pm Sun** 🚊 4, 9, 16, 24, 25 ♿ **excellent**

Concertgebouw (3, B4)
This world-famous concert hall (see also p31) with near-perfect acoustics attracts renowned international soloists, orchestras and chamber groups, while the resident Royal Concertgebouw Orchestra is one of the world's best. Free lunchtime concerts are held at 12.30pm Wednesday.

☎ 671 83 45 (recording in Dutch), 675 44 11 🖥 www.concertgebouw .nl ✉ Concertgebouwplein 2-6 € €12-60 ☟ box office 10am-8.15pm (tickets for that evening's performance after 7pm) 🚊 3, 5, 12 ♿ **excellent**

Muziekcentrum De IJsbreker (1, D4)
Overlooking the Amstel, this contemporary music centre stages challenging, avant-garde symphonies and other arty, international compositions. It's due to move in early 2005 with the Bimhuis (p90), though this date has been put back a couple of times already.
☎ 693 90 93 🖥 www .ysbreker.nl ✉ Weesperzijde 23 € €2-13 ☟ box office 9.30am-5.30pm (from 7.45pm on performance night) 🚊 3 ♿ **poor**

Muziektheater (2, E8)
The Muziektheater (aka the Stopera, p34) is a massive, plush concert hall

MARTIN MOOS

Built in 1888 – the lyre-bedecked Concertgebouw

boasting programs of top local and international ballets and operas. They also have regular modern-dance performances. Book ahead if either of the two resident companies, the Netherlands Opera and the Netherlands National Ballet, is performing.
☎ 625 54 55 🖥 www .hetmuziektheater.nl ✉ Waterlooplein 22 € €13-40 for ballet, €22-63 for opera ☟ box office 10am-6pm Mon-Sat, 11.30am-6pm Sun 🚊 4, 9, 14 Ⓜ Waterlooplein ♿ **excellent**

Church Concerts
Worship at the altar of good music at one of the concerts held in the city's many monumental churches. Organ recitals are of course held in every church that's got a big one, but there are also regular choral and chamber music performances. The best are at the **Engelse Kerk** (p31; ☎ 624 9665) in the Begijnhof; the **Nieuwe Kerk** (p33; ☎ 626 8168); the **Noorderkerk** (p33; ☎ 427 61 63); the **Oude Kerk** (p13; ☎ 625 82 84); and the **Westerkerk** (p23; ☎ 624 77 66). Ring each for times, or check with the **AUB** (☎ 0900-0191).

COFFEESHOPS

Da 'erb is tolerated in the Netherlands like nowhere else. Contrary to what you might have heard, though, cannabis products are illegal; the Dutch police simply turn a blind eye to soft drugs for personal use, meaning you can carry up to 5g without a care in the world.

You can buy dope hassle-free in more than 180 registered coffeeshops, but there are a few rules: buy from coffeeshops and never from a street dealer; exercise courtesy when smoking in bars (most places don't mind, but you must check before lighting up); and finally, go easy on that first joint, because the dope here is seriously strong.

Barney's (2, B1)
Barney's is the place to head for a joint with your morning juice. It also does a roaring trade in all-day American, Irish and vegetarian breakfasts. The interior, a mystifying mix of *Lord of the Rings*–style fantasy and New Age mysticism, is best appreciated after a spliff. ☎ 625 97 61 ✉ Haarlemmerstraat 102 ⏱ 7.30am-8pm 🚋 1, 2, 5, 13, 17 ♿ poor

Greenhouse (2, D5)
This extremely popular Indonesian-inspired coffeeshop has been the recipient of many awards at the

> ## Top Places to Puff on a Joint
> - Vondelpark (p18)
> - The terrace of NEMO (p27)
> - Just before a tour of the red-light district
> - IJburg beach (p17)

annual High Times festival. The quality Dutch-grown product and selection of imported weed draws in the connoisseurs. It's also an entertaining place for a beer, even if you're not torching up a doobie. ☎ 627 17 39 ✉ Oudezijds Voorburgwal 191 ⏱ 9am-1am (to 3am Fri & Sat) 🚋 4, 9, 16, 24, 25 ♿ poor

Kadinsky (2, B6)
Well decorated and well situated, this popular joint is just off the Spui. Staffed by friendly types who won't give the drug illiterati any attitude, the space cake here is renowned, for its effects of course, but also for tasting like cake and not cardboard. ☎ 624 70 23 ✉ Rosmarijnsteeg 9 ⏱ 10am-1am 🚋 1, 2, 5 ♿ poor

Breakfast at Barney's — all day long

Rokerij (5, C6)

Rokerij is a cheery find in the glum Leidseplein area. Seen by candlelight, the colourful Indian decoration works well and the staff – eerily for a coffeeshop – aren't jerks. They also sell booze.
☎ 422 66 43 ✉ Lange Leidsedwarsstraat 41 🕑 10am-1am (to 3am Fri & Sat) 🚊 1, 2, 5, 7, 10 ♿ good

Siberie (2, C2)

A bright, spotless coffeeshop completely lacking in the Place-for-Stoner-Dudes vibe that many other places have in spades. There are regular jazz performances, DJs on summer weekends, and a free astrologer every Sunday evening from 6.30-8.30pm. Siberie, which turned 20 in 2004, is one of the city's best places to suck on some smoke.
☎ 623 59 09 🖥 www .siberie.nl ✉ Brouwers-gracht 11 🕑 11am-11pm (to midnight Fri & Sat) 🚊 1, 2, 5, 13, 17 ♿ good

The Grass Is Always Greener

Let's get something straight: Amsterdam's coffeeshops are in the cannabis business. If you enter simply looking for an espresso and a slice of cake, you're in for a big surprise.

In 1976 the Netherlands allowed coffeeshops as a way of separating marijuana smokers from those using harder drugs. It worked: in 2002, Britain had 250,000 'problem' hard-drug addicts in a population of 60 million (or 0.42%), compared to the Netherlands, with 25,000 out of 17 million (0.15%).

Amsterdam's 300 coffeeshops attract locals and tourists from all walks of life. Some are filled with grungy backpackers, others with knitwear-clad middle-aged men. There's even a couple for groovy gay boys. All display a smokers' menu detailing the price per gram (it's generally sold in 1g bags) and country of origin. Prices (€8 to €16 per gram) depend on rarity and strength. Most coffeeshops also sell rolled joints for around €3. Ask staff about the product's potency and the sort of high to expect.

Space cakes and cookies are also sold, but you have to ask for them as they're not on the menu, mainly because tourists are unused to them. Ask the staff how much you should eat and how long it will take for the effect to kick in, as it can take over an hour. Just in case, here's a handy phrase: 'Ik denk dat ik te veel spacecake heb opgegeten' (I think I ate too much space cake.)

Those on their cannabis training wheels are advised not to combine booze and dope because the results can be unpredictable. You won't grow an extra head, but you're more likely to feel morose or sick. And if you overdo it, drink or eat something with sugar in it.

A hot choice: Siberie, one of Amsterdam's most famous coffeeshops

GAY & LESBIAN AMSTERDAM

Amsterdam decriminalised homosexuality in the 1800s and celebrated the world's first gay marriage in 2002, and its hedonistic gay scene is Europe's most liberal. Many think of Amsterdam as the planet's gay capital. Venues are everywhere and apart from those listed here there's a plethora of weekly queer club nights held at larger straight clubs. Club nights are generally not long-lived; ask at friendly bars such as Getto or Sappho or at the Other Side coffeeshop (see p97). *Gay News Amsterdam* (www.gaynews.nl), in English and Dutch, is available free in gay-friendly venues and has information on both gay and lesbian venues and events. Otherwise, contact the **Gay & Lesbian Switchboard** (☎ 623 65 65) for the latest hot spot.

Though Amsterdam is Europe's most tolerant society for just about everything, that hasn't translated to a plethora of women's bars. Still, the bars that are here (see p97) are wonderful.

FOR GAY MEN

Argos (2, D4)

Hidden behind totally blacked-out front windows, Amsterdam's oldest leather bar is for serious players only, as evidenced by its constantly packed basement darkroom. There's a raucous front bar and a steady stream of porn playing on screens in the rear bar.

☎ 662 65 95 ⌨ Warmoesstraat 95 € free
☽ 10pm-3am (to 4am Fri & Sat) 🚊 4, 9, 16, 24, 25 ♿ fair

Cockring (2, D4)

Leather boys of all ages head to this busy nightclub, famous throughout Europe for its cruisey darkroom. Get sweaty beforehand, either on the dance floor to techno and house, or while watching sizzling strip shows. On Sunday afternoons Cockring hosts sex parties.

☎ 623 96 04 ⌨ www .clubcockring.com ✉ Warmoesstraat 96 € free-€5
☽ 11pm-4am (to 5am Fri & Sat) 🚊 4, 9, 16, 24, 25 ♿ good

De Trut (5, A5)

De Trut makes Sunday fun for queer Amsterdam. This alternative club held in the basement of an industrial squat fills up quickly so arrive before 10.30pm. Expect hard techno, house and arty multimedia performances.

✉ Bilderdijkstraat 165
€ €3 ☽ Sun 11pm-4am
🚊 3, 7, 12, 17
♿ excellent

Entre Nous (2, C8)

You may find you need the soothing tones of the red wallpaper and slick furnishings at this understated bar after a visit across the road to the outrageous Montmartre (see p96). It gets unbelievably packed late on Friday and Saturday nights.

☎ 623 17 00 ✉ Halvemaansteeg 14 ☽ 8pm-3am (to 4am Fri & Sat)
🚊 1, 2, 4, 5, 9, 16, 24, 25 ♿ good

Exit (3, D1)

Exit is a sure bet for a big night out for beautiful gay boys, with its great selection of bars over three levels. There's a dance floor playing pop, one playing R&B and one with house.

Take Pride

The first weekend in August is reserved for Amsterdam Pride (www.amsterdam pride.nl), the city's annual knees-up for the gay and lesbian community and the Netherlands' biggest gay event. The three-day party includes a gay float parade on the canals, including up to 80 boats, and street parties and performances that take place right round the city.

Queer Quarters

Busy districts for gay men include:

- **Reguliersdwarsstraat** (2, B8) Amsterdam's most famous gay establishments line the street. They attract hip and beautiful men who cruise and schmooze.
- **Amstel & Rembrandtplein** (2, D8) Real queen territory with a selection of interesting bars; some are camp (Dutch pop-song sing-alongs), some cloney (moustache city), and some refined and quiet (businessmen).
- **Warmoesstraat** (2, D4) In the red-light district, and catering to lovers of leather, rubber, darkrooms and hard-core porn. A few gay bars have also opened on nearby Zeedijk in recent years.

The darkroom downstairs sees constant action.
☎ 625 87 88 ⊠ Reguliersdwarsstraat 42 € free-€5 ✆ 11pm-4am (to 5am Fri & Sat) 🚊 1, 2, 4, 5, 14, 16, 24, 25 ♿ excellent

Getto (2, D4)

Creating a bar where everyone will feel comfortable is difficult, but Getto has pulled it off. Locals know it's a relaxing place to start a night of merry mayhem in Warmoesstraat. They have a daily cocktail happy hour from 5-7pm and also do great food.
☎ 421 51 51 🖥 www .getto.nl ⊠ Warmoesstraat 51 € free ✆ Tue 7pm-1am, Wed-Sat 4pm-1am, Sun 1pm-midnight 🚊 4, 9, 16, 24, 25 ♿ poor

Montmartre (2, D8)

This kingdom of camp is quite an experience. Picture the entire cast and crew of the last Eurovision packed into a tiny bar, and you're almost there. The mixed gay crowd shake their groove things to disco classics on the dance floor till late into the night, and staff and patrons are known to break into Dutch ballads and glam pop songs.
☎ 620 76 22 ⊠ Halvemaansteeg 17 € free ✆ 5pm-1am (to 3am Fri & Sat) 🚊 4, 9, 14 ♿ excellent

Soho (3, D1)

This constantly packed split-level bar is kitschly decorated (imagine ye olde-worlde English library on the *Titanic*)

Reguliersdwarsstraat: regular cruising ground for gay men

RICHARD NEBESKY

Get inside the Other Side

Sappho (3, D1)
Friday is the big night at Sappho, when this laid-back bar fairly teems with some of the Western world's sexiest women. Men are welcome but they must be accompanied by a woman. ☎ 423 15 09 🖳 www .sappho.nl ✉ Vijzelstraat 103 € free ☽ Sun-Thu 3pm-1am, Fri & Sat to 3am 🚊 16, 24, 25 ♿ excellent

Vivelavie (2, D8)
Vivelavie is the lesbian bar you head for if (and many would say only if) you're not quite ready to stop drinking yet. Friendly bar staff and the wonderful terrace in summer make it a sceney place for a drink until late. ☎ 624 01 14 ✉ Amstelstraat 7 € free ☽ 3pm-1am (to 3am Fri & Sat) 🚊 4, 9, 14 ♿ excellent

and attracts a young crowd who like to strut their stuff on the dance floor. ☎ 330 44 00 ✉ Regu-liersdwarsstraat 36 € free ☽ 8pm-3am Mon-Thu, to 4am Fri & Sat, 5pm-3am Sun 🚊 1, 2, 4, 5, 14, 16, 24, 25 ♿ excellent

The Other Side (2, B8)
This gay-run coffeeshop plays a mix of disco, funk and soul and sells hash, weed and energy drinks. It's bright, airy and a whole heap of fun, and as much a lesbian venue as gay male. ☎ 421 10 14 ✉ Reguliersdwarsstraat 6 € free ☽ 11am-1am 🚊 1, 2, 5, 16, 24, 25 ♿ good

FOR WOMEN
Saarein II (5, B4)
Saarein II was a feminist movement focal point in the 1970s, and has re-mained popular ever since. Set in a beautiful 17th-century building, Sareein II welcomes gay and straight men and women, though it's primarily a lesbian meeting place. It has a great restaurant, reading table and pool table. ☎ 623 49 01 ✉ Elandsstraat 119 € free ☽ 5pm-1am Tue-Thu & Sun, to 2am Fri & Sat 🚊 7, 10, 17 ♿ excellent

Join the serene sisterhood at Saarein II

All Steamed Up
There are two gay saunas in town, run by the same owners: Thermos Day Sauna and Thermos Night Sauna. The **day sauna** (☎ 623 91 58; www.thermos.nl; Raamstraat 33; admission €18; ☽ noon-11pm Mon-Fri, to 10pm Sat, 11am-10pm Sun) is a sprawling place with porn movies, darkrooms, roof deck and restaurant. When it shuts, head for the nearby **night sauna** (☎ 623 49 36; Kerkstraat 58-60; admission €18; ☽ 11pm-8am Sun-Fri, to 10am Sat), which is really just one big series of sweaty darkrooms.

SPORT

Football (soccer) is the Netherlands' sport of choice, but there are other sports for the keen observer to get fired up about.

Football

The Netherlands' top team, the Jewish-backed Ajax, plays in the massive **ArenA Stadium** (1, C5; ☎ 311 13 33; Arena Boulevard 29, Bijlmer) from September to June, with a winter break from Christmas to February. The high-tech complex, seating 52,000 spectators, features a snazzy retractable roof and an interactive museum complete with paraphernalia, films and some 3-D animation. Games usually take place Saturday evening and Sunday afternoon.

Hockey

The Dutch (field) hockey team is among the world's best. The season runs between September and May. Contact **Hockey Club Hurley** (☎ 619 02 33; Nieuwe Kalfjeslaan 21, Amsterdamse Bos), for information and to find out when internationals are being held at the 7000-seat Wagener Stadium.

Korfball

A cross between netball, volleyball and basketball, korfball often elicits paroxysms of giggles from first-time spectators. It's played by mixed-sex teams who attempt to throw a ball into the opposing team's hoop: players can only mark opponents of the same sex. There's a huge local club scene and a long season that incorporates both field and indoor games. Contact the **Amsterdam Sport Council** (☎ 552 24 90) for further information.

ArenA Stadium, home to top football team, Ajax, and top venue for blockbuster concerts

Sleeping

Space has always been a sought-after commodity in Amsterdam, something you'll appreciate when looking for a hotel. Hotels tend to have few rooms (anything with more than 20 rooms is big) and rooms are often small, especially in less expensive places. Posh hotels far outweigh the cheap, and in spring and summer all rooms get snapped up quickly, so it's imperative to book ahead.

It's definitely worth paying more for something central so you can enjoy the nightlife without resorting to night buses or taxis. This doesn't mean you have to stay within the canal belt, however; accommodation in the Museumplein area or around the Vondelpark, for instance, is a short walk from the lively Leidseplein area.

Room Rates
The categories in this guide indicate the cost per night of a standard double room.
Deluxe   over €200
Top End   €130-200
Mid-Range   €70-130
Budget   under €70

Top-end and deluxe hotels all have rooms with private bathrooms, whereas this is less common in cheaper places. However, hotels in the mid-range and budget price bracket usually include breakfast.

Many hotels have narrow, ladder-like stairs and no lifts (elevators), which can make them inaccessible for some. Even top-end places might not have a lift: ring ahead and ask.

Ask about parking if you're travelling by car. Parking is almost always a major problem and the most you'll get is a street-parking permit – with all the atte ndant headaches and security risks – or a referral to the nearest security-watched garage (at up to €30 a day.). The top-end and deluxe hotels have their own parking, but like to be warned in advance.

The efficient www.bookings.nl is your best online hotel-booking option; bookings are free and you receive confirmation in seconds. If you're not so well prepared, same-day hotel bookings can be made at **VVV** (☎ 201 88 00; Centraal Station; 🕑 9am-5pm); **GWK** (☎ 627 27 27; Centraal Station; 🕑 7.45am-10pm) and **Netherlands Reservation Centre** (☎ 070-419 55 00; www.hotelres.nl; Postbus 404, 2260 AK Leidschendam), where bookings are free.

Pull up a pew at this former monastery's bar (Hotel Arena, p102)

DELUXE

717 (5, C6)

Elton John and Yves Saint Laurent have been among guests at Amsterdam's swankiest hotel (rates start at €375). Its eight hyper-plush rooms are huge by any standards, boasting soaring ceilings, graceful decorations and bathrooms as big as some European principalities. Rates include breakfast, afternoon tea and as much booze as you can drink.
☎ 427 07 17
🖳 www.717hotel.nl
✉ Prinsengracht 717
🚊 1, 2, 5 ♿ poor

Amstel InterContinental Hotel (3, F3)

Visiting heads of state: sack your assistant if they fail to check you into the Amstel. Brad and George are just two in a long line of members of high society who have flocked to the Amstel since it opened in 1867. It's known as the Netherlands' finest hotel.
☎ 622 60 60 🖳 www .interconti.com ✉ Professor Tulpplein 1 🚊 6, 7, 10 ♿ excellent ✗ La Rive 🛗

Blakes Amsterdam (5, C4)

Beautiful courtyard, beautiful rooms, beautiful bar, beautiful people – welcome to the world of the über-chic. A conversion of several 17th-century town houses, this utterly glamorous hotel is a designer's delight, much like its two London siblings.
☎ 530 20 10 🖳 www .slh.com/blakes ✉ Keizersgracht 384 🚊 1, 2, 5 ♿ excellent ✗ Blakes Restaurant

The Grand (2, C6)

Michael Jackson and other nonindicted famous folk choose to stay here, partly for the luxury, but also for the heavy-duty security measures on offer. This palatial building was the town hall from 1808 to 1987, hence the spacious courtyard, grandiose stairwells and cavernous rooms, all with excellent canal views. Hunt out Karel Appel's *Inquisitive Children*, painted to repay a tax debt to the city.
☎ 555 31 11 🖳 www .thegrand.nl ✉ Oudezijds Voorburgwal 197 🚊 4, 9, 16, 24, 25 ♿ excellent ✗ Café Roux 🛗

Grand Hotel Krasnapolsky (2, C5)

On Dam Square opposite Koninklijk Paleis and the Nationaal Monument, the elegant Krasnapolsky is a town monument in its own right. With 461 ultra-plush rooms, the historic hotel is also a colossus. If you're planning a stay of two weeks or longer, their 36 luxurious apartments – from €110 per night – are very reasonably priced.
☎ 554 91 11 🖳 www .nh-hotels.com ✉ Dam 9 🚊 4, 9, 16, 24, 25 ♿ excellent ✗ French, Japanese & Bedouin restaurants; the Winter Garden restaurant 🛗

Hotel de l'Europe (2, C7)

This grandiose pile has a wonderful location and commanding Amstel views. The hotel was owned by beer magnate Freddy Heineken

until his death in 2002, and a good part of his US$2.6 billion fortune appears to have been spent on the hotel's opulent furniture.
☎ 531 17 77 🖳 www .leurope.nl ✉ Nieuwe Doelenstraat 2-8 🚊 4, 9, 14, 16, 24 ♿ fair ✗ Excelsior Restaurant 🛗

Lloyd Hotel (1, E3)

Originally built in 1921 as a hotel for migrants en route to the Americas, this unique hotel opened in August 2004. The Lloyd aims to introduce Dutch culture to its guests and its guests' culture to the Dutch! The remarkable array of rooms ranges from one- to five-star, and includes tiny bedrooms with little more than a double bed up to utterly grand, sumptuous rooms fit for a rock star.
☎ 561 36 36 🖳 www .lloydhotel.com ✉ Oostelijke Handelskade 34; 🚊 IJburg tram from Centraal Station ♿ excellent ✗ Sloom & Snel

Park your bike at Blakes Amsterdam

RICHARD NEBESKY

TOP END

Hotel Ambassade (2, A7)

This stylish hotel, spread over 10 canal houses, uses a literary linchpin as its drawcard: there is a library of more than 1500 books, many signed by authors who have stayed there. The tastefully appointed rooms are all decked out with antique furniture.
☎ 555 02 22 ⌨ www .ambassade-hotel.nl ✉ Herengracht 341 🚊 1, 2, 5 ♿ excellent ✕ ♨

Find a famous author at this literary hotel

Bilderberg Jan Luyken (3, B3)

On a quiet street between the Rijksmuseum and the Vondelpark, this refined boutique hotel exudes an air of unobtrusive wealth. Rooms are tastefully decorated, and its location in peaceful Jan Luijken-straat makes it perfect for art groupies headed for the Van Gogh Museum and the Rijksmuseum.
☎ 573 07 30 ⌨ www .janluyken.nl ✉ Jan Luijkenstraat 58 🚊 2, 5 ♿ fair ♨

Black Tulip Hotel (2, E3)

All good hotel rooms are spotlessly clean, have cable TV and an en suite. The Black Tulip's classy rooms have all that, plus bondage slings, fisting chairs and whipping benches as well. Regardless of the bondage gear on offer, the rooms are impeccably decorated at this exclusively gay-male hotel.
☎ 427 09 33 ⌨ www .blacktulip.nl ✉ Gelder-skade 16 🚊 4, 9, 16, 24, 25 ♿ poor

Canal House (2, A3)

These two handsome 17th-century buildings are as charming as they are well located. The Irish owners love their hotel, with its ornate ceilings and scores of antiques, and it comes through in the rooms: old-fashioned and extremely comfortable, just like the Victorian-style bar and garden.
☎ 622 51 82 ⌨ www .canalhouse.nl ✉ Keizers-gracht 148 🚊 13, 14, 17 ♿ poor ✕ ♨

Hotel Estherea (2, A6)

Opened during WWII by a mother and her three daughters, Estherea was originally a tiny inn. Today it's still family owned but spread over six luxurious 17th-century canal houses. Each of its 70 rooms is individual and spotless, and 20 of them have great views over the Singel.
☎ 624 51 46 ⌨ www .estherea.nl ✉ Singel 303-309 🚊 1, 2, 5 ♿ fair ✕ ♨

Hotel Vondel (3, B2)

In a very quiet street five minutes' walk from both the Rijksmuseum and Leidseplein, this beautiful and popular hotel has 70 rooms — all bright, spacious and decorated with genteel class. There's also an exqui-site courtyard garden.
☎ 612 01 20 ⌨ www .bookings.nl/hotels /vondel ✉ Vondelstraat 28-30 🚊 1, 3, 5, 6, 12 ♿ good ✕ ♨

't hotel (2, A4)

Quiet and understated, 't hotel is a genuine find. In a 17th-century canal house with eight rooms, the styl-ish furniture matches the stunning rooms. Breakfast is served in a delightful down-stairs dining room. Book room seven (around €140 a night): it's a sun-filled space with a gabled roof and large windows overlooking the canal.
☎ 422 27 41 ⌨ www .bookings.nl/hotels/thotel ✉ Leliegracht 18 🚊 13, 14, 17 ♿ poor ✕ ♨

MID-RANGE

Amstel Botel (4, A2)

This converted ferry, two minutes' walk east of Centraal Station, is attractive for its price, location and mod cons. All rooms cost around €80, have a tiny shower and toilet, TV and phone and are very clean. But they're as small and charmless as you'd expect of a ferry. It's a reliable place if everything else is full.

☎ 626 42 47 🖥 www .amstelbotel.com ✉ Oosterdokskade 2-4 🚊 1, 2, 4, 5, 9, 13, 16, 17, 24, 25 ♿ excellent ✗ ⚤

Atlas (3, A3)

In a quiet spot not far from Vondelpark you'll find this stunning Art Deco villa. The plain rooms (doubles from €110) are pleasant enough, and have modern bathrooms, but it's the lovely building, exclusive neighbourhood and professional staff that make Atlas a good choice.

☎ 676 63 36 🖥 www .atlashotel.nl ✉ Van Eeghenstraat 64 🚊 2 ♿ excellent ✗ Atlas ⚤

Hotel Acro (3, B3)

In a prime spot for art lovers, close to the Rijksmuseum, the Van Gogh Museum and the Stedelijk, the Acro has simple but ultra-comfortable and spotless en-suite rooms. Located in one of the area's prettiest streets, it's a good choice, especially for the low room rates (doubles from €90).

☎ 662 55 38 🖥 www .acro-hotel.nl ✉ Jan Luijkenstraat 44 🚊 2, 5 ♿ excellent ✗ ⚤

Where to Stay if You're Gay
- Black Tulip Hotel (p101)
- Golden Bear (p103)
- Hotel Aero (below)
- Hotel Orfeo (p104)
- Hotel Quentin (pictured, see below)
- Liliane's Home (p103)

MARTIN MOOS

Hotel Aero (2, A9)

Aero is a popular gay hotel in the middle of the action not far from Leidseplein, with clean, simple doubles from €70. It's good value for the district, though some rooms facing the street can be noisy.

☎ 622 77 28 🖥 www .aerohotel.nl ✉ Kerkstraat 49 🚊 1, 2, 5, 11 ✗ ♿ poor

Hotel Arena (1, E4)

Once a monastery, and not so long ago a huge hostel, Arena was converted in 2000 into a stylish hotel, complete with a bar, restaurant and nightclub. The rooms, starting at €125, are great places to stay. All have polished wood floors and minimalist furniture, and most have a private bathroom.

☎ 850 24 00 🖥 www .hotelarena.nl ✉ 's-Gravesandestraat 51 🚊 3, 6, 10 ♿ excellent ✗ café, bar & restaurant

Hotel de Filosoof (1, C4)

This delightful hotel welcomes all manner of epistemologists and metaphysicists to its 38 small but comfortable rooms, each dedicated to a philosopher, writer or thinker. Some rooms, such

as the Wittgenstein, are festooned with lush furniture. Others, such as the Zen room, are spartan and serene. The Marx (Karl, not Groucho) is suitably utilitarian.

☎ 683 30 13 🖥 www .hotelfilosoof.nl ✉ Anna van den Vondelstraat 6 🚊 1, 6 ♿ fair ✗ ⚤

Hotel Quentin (5, B6)

Welcoming to gays, lesbians and heteros, this tidy and somewhat eccentric 32-room hotel attracts plenty of artists performing at Leidseplein theatres. There's no lift, and rooms in the upper floors can be a bit cramped, but the laconic staff are welcoming and good fun.

☎ 626 21 87 🖥 www .quentinhotel.com ✉ Leidsekade 89 🚊 1, 2, 5 ♿ poor ✗

Hotel The Crown (2, E4)

A dependable option in the red-light district, its simple, tidy doubles are great value for the location at €80; they also do quads and even six-person rooms.

☎ 626 96 64 🖥 www .hotelthecrown.com ✉ Oudezijds Voorburgwal 21 🚊 4, 9, 16, 24, 25 ♿ fair ✗

Hotel van Onna (5, B2)

It's a cruel joke, really it is. You've scored an immaculate room overlooking a canal in the prettiest part of Amsterdam. Then, as night falls, church rage sets in: nearby Westerkerk's bells peal every half-hour (they stop from 1am to 6am). Light sleepers should avoid the front rooms, but otherwise this ultra-friendly hotel is an absolute find. No credit cards.

☎ 626 58 01 🖳 www .vanonna.nl ✉ Bloemgracht 102-108 🚊 13, 14, 17 ♿ fair ✕ ♨

Liliane's Home (1, E4)

The sole women-only establishment in town, this place is really a private home. But its nine nicely appointed rooms are a steal at €100, including a cooked breakfast delivered to your room. It isn't geared for walk-ins, so book in advance. The managers can be gruff but they're soft-hearted.

Perfectly named for the location: the Seven Bridges hotel

☎ 627 40 06 ✉ Sarphatistraat 119 🚊 1, 2, 5 ♿ poor

Seven Bridges (3, E2)

Here, quite possibly, is Amsterdam's best hotel. Why do we love it so? Let us count the ways: affordable rooms (doubles from €110 including breakfast) with antique furniture, owners who take pride in their hotel, views over a stunning canal, breakfast served on fine china in your room, and a prime location near Rembrandtplein. Book well in advance.

☎ 623 13 29 ✉ Reguliersgracht 31 🚊 4, 9, 14, 16, 24, 25 ♿ poor ♨

Zosa Hotel (2, D5)

The six rooms at the Zosa Hotel might be small, but they make up for it with class. Each is individually decorated (one à la Rembrandt), and the slightly larger front rooms overlook the canal. The owner's top choice is room five for its fine views over the back garden.

☎ 330 62 41 🖳 www .zosa-online.com ✉ Kloveniersburgwal 20 🚊 4, 9, 17, 24, 25 ♿ poor ✕

BUDGET

The Bulldog Hotel (2, D5)

Budget travellers would be nuts to stay anywhere else. The staff are friendly and helpful and the dorm rooms (€22 per person) are the best we've ever seen, brilliantly designed with two bathrooms, lockers and simple but comfortable beds; the comfortable doubles (€77) are equally good. Breakfast is included.

☎ 620 38 22 🖳 www .bulldog.nl ✉ Oudezijds Voorburgwal 216 🚊 4, 9, 16, 24, 25 ✕ ♿ good

Euphemia Hotel (3, D2)

Set in a former monastery, this hotel is in a quiet street inside the canal belt. Its institutional layout makes the hotel a bit sterile, as do the unhelpful staff, but location and price make it tempting.

☎ 622 90 45 🖳 www .euphemiahotel.com ✉ Fokke Simonszstraat 1 🚊 6, 7, 10, 16, 24, 25 ♿ fair ✕ ♨

Golden Bear (5, C6)

The sizable rooms in this friendly, exclusively gay hotel

are very comfortable – all singles have double beds – and good value for the area. Most rooms have an en suite.

☎ 624 47 85 🖳 www .goldenbear.nl ✉ Kerkstraat 37 🚊 1, 2, 5 ♿ poor ✕

Hans Brinker Budget Hotel (3, C2)

Taking its name from the boy who plugged a dyke with his finger, this huge hotel and hostel plugs the gap in the market for travellers who want clean rooms, good beds and minimal fuss (its slogan: 'no car park, no room service, no minibars, no hole in your pocket'). It's well located and has a great bar and club downstairs.

☎ 622 06 87 ⌨ www .hans-brinker.com ✉ Kerkstraat 136 🚊 1, 2, 4, 5, 9, 14 ♿ excellent ✗ ♨

Hotel Bema (3, B4)

Who cares that the furniture doesn't match? At this slightly dishevelled hotel by the Concertgebouw, you'll get a courteous welcome and a clean, spacious room. Ask for one out the back, as the trams get noisy.

☎ 679 13 96 ⌨ www .hotel-bema.demon.nl ✉ Concertgebouwplein 19b 🚊 3, 5, 12, 16 ♿ poor ✗ ♨

Hotel Beursstraat (2, D4)

Near the Oude Kerk in the red-light district, this is a no-fuss, low-service hotel. Don't expect a whole lotta lovin' when you're checking in or out – just low prices and tidy, simple rooms, most of which have a private bath.

☎ 626 37 01 ⌨ www .channels.nl/amster-dam/beursho.html ✉ Beursstraat 7 🚊 4, 9, 16, 24, 25 ♿ fair ✗

Hotel Hortus (4, A5)

A relaxed little place in a side street in the north-eastern corner of the canal belt, Hotel Hortus is directly across from the Hortus Botanicus. The clientele includes young, happy smokers. Doubles are small but good value, a continental breakfast is included, and there's a common kitchen, and nice lounge.

☎ 625 99 96 ⌨ www .hotelhortus.com ✉ Plantage Parklaan 8 🚊 9, 14 ♿ fair ✗

Hotel Orfeo (3, C2)

Very friendly and laid-back, this gay hotel is near the nightlife hub of Leidseplein. All rooms have TV, telephone and minibar, and there's a fun lounge to hang out in.

☎ 623 13 47 ⌨ www .hotelorfeo.com ✉ Leidsekruisstraat 14 🚊 1, 2, 5, 7, 10 ♿ poor ✗

Hotel Prinsenhof (3, E1)

This is one of the most reasonably priced options in town. Off lively Utrechtse-straat, its spotless rooms are well appointed, beds comfortable and staff helpful and professional. The pricier attic rooms (€90) have high ceilings and exposed beams. Book well ahead.

☎ 623 17 72 ⌨ www .hotelprinsenhof.com ✉ Prinsengracht 810 🚊 4 ♿ fair ✗ ♨

Hotel Rembrandt (4, A5)

In the leafy residential area near the Artis Zoo and botanical gardens, the Rembrandt's doubles (marginally outside the budget category, starting at €70 a night) are great value. The morning repast alone makes a visit worthwhile. Breakfast in the stunning, wood-panelled breakfast area, which features 17th-century paintings on linen-covered walls, is a treat.

☎ 627 27 14 ⌨ www .hotelrembrandt.nl ✉ Plantage Middenlaan 17 🚊 9, 14 ♿ good ✗ ♨

Windows designed by CoBrA group artists for the Hans Brinker Budget Hotel (p103)

About Amsterdam

HISTORY

The oldest archaeological finds in Amsterdam date from Roman times, though the Romans didn't bother settling the waterlogged swamplands in the northern parts of Holland. Pioneering peasants living on the banks of the River IJ began to venture into this wilderness, building the first dams around 1150. Soon there emerged a fishing village known as Aemstelredamme ('dam built across the River Amstel') at what is now Dam Square, and in 1275 the village of Amsterdam was officially born.

Focusing on trade with Germany and the Baltic cities, the village of Amsterdam grew rapidly into a maritime city. Building dykes and pooling resources among firms that financed resources and shared risks, the new trading city undertook audacious ventures without fear of losing everything. By the 1490s, nearly two-thirds of ships bound to the Baltic Sea were from Holland (and most of these had owners from Amsterdam).

Independent Republic

During the Reformation in the 15th century, the stern Calvinist movement took hold in the Low Countries. This was key to the region's struggle against the fanatical rule of the Catholic Philip II of Spain, who had acquired these 17 provinces and ran them in true colonial fashion. In 1578 Calvinist brigands captured Amsterdam in a bloodless coup, and the northern provinces declared themselves an independent republic.

The Golden Age

When Antwerp (now in Belgium) was taken by the Spaniards in the late 16th century, merchants, skippers and artisans flocked to Amsterdam, and a new moneyed society emerged, trade-based but intellectual. The world's first regular newspaper was printed here in 1618. Persecuted Jews from Portugal and Spain also fled to Amsterdam; they knew of trade routes to the West and East Indies, introduced the diamond industry (fed by Brazilian gems) and made Amsterdam a tobacco centre. The city grew apace: the population quadrupled to 220,000 in the 100 years to 1700. The Dutch dominated in sea trade over other European powers, giving them a virtual monopoly on North Sea fishing and Arctic whaling.

Dressed to kill: an 18th-century Dutch ship

Wealthy Decline

By the late 1600s, Holland didn't have the resources to match the growing might of France and England. Dutch merchants began to invest their fortunes in secure ventures, rather than in sea voyages to unknown lands. The result was stagnation, with wealth created via interest rates. The mighty United East India Company, which once controlled European trade with Asia, went bankrupt in 1800.

The 19th Century

Amsterdam shook off its torpor when Holland's first railway opened in 1839. Major infrastructure projects formed the backbone of Amsterdam's economy. Canal links to the North Sea and the Rhine River helped the city benefit from the Industrial Revolution. The harbour was expanded, the diamond industry boomed and Amsterdam's population passed the half-million mark by 1900.

WWII & the Post-War Period

During WWII, Amsterdam experienced war for the first time in almost four centuries. The harsh winter of 1944–45 brought severe famine and thousands died. After WWII, with US aid and the discovery of new natural-gas fields, the city's growth resumed.

Amsterdam Today

The economic growth of the 1950s led to a cultural revolution in the '60s that swept away the days of autocratic government. Grandiose housing schemes were hatched and many old neighbourhoods were demolished. By the '90s the city had changed radically: the centre was now dominated by a booming service industry and white-collar professionals. Amsterdam won back the economic status that had eluded it since the Golden Age. In national polls it remains the most popular (and most expensive) Dutch city to live in. Yet, despite creeping yuppification, Amsterdam retains its easy cosmopolitan feel thanks to its multicultural mix. Nearly half the city's residents come from abroad, the largest groups hailing from Surinam, Morocco and Turkey.

Cleaning the Canals

In the 17th century, the Amstel locks began being flushed daily of human waste, household garbage, butchers' offal (and much else). There were vocal protests from maids when the flushing began; they were afraid they'd lose their jobs due to falling filth levels. Today, the canals are still flushed daily. Between 7pm and 8.30pm, 40 sluices in the city centre are closed and an enormous pumping station on Zeeburg (an island in the city's east) pumps 600,000 cu metres of water from the IJsselmeer into the canals. The sluices are then opened and the water flows into the River IJ. Despite this, 60-odd fish species – saltwater, freshwater and brackish types – still manage to survive.

Cycling through Amsterdamse Bos along a freshly flushed canal

ENVIRONMENT

Green issues are paramount in Western Europe's most densely populated country, which has 16 million people in a far smaller space than the Republic of Ireland (which has approximately 5.5 million people). The canals are cleaner today than they've ever been, and use of environmentally friendly natural gas has cleared the air. Industrial pollution is kept firmly in check with some of the strictest regulations in the world.

The inner city has become a much more pleasant place for pedestrians since the mid-1980s thanks to the council's efforts to curb the number of cars in town. The number of parking spaces is strongly curtailed and cars are actively discouraged.

GOVERNMENT & POLITICS

With Belgium and Luxembourg, the Netherlands belongs to the Benelux, a three-country free-trade area that served as a model for the EU, of which the Dutch are founding members. Amsterdam is the Dutch capital but, confusingly, Parliament and the seat of government are in The Hague. Queen Beatrix is formally the head of state, but her function is largely symbolic as the Netherlands has been a parliamentary democracy since the mid-19th century.

Amsterdam has been a left-wing city ever since its residents won the vote. Amsterdam's city council and municipal executive oversee the city's 16 districts (each with its own district council and executive committee) and run the central city within the canal belt and the western harbour area. Its 45 council members are elected every four years, while the mayor is appointed by the Crown for a period of six years. The districts have a great deal of autonomy, hence services can vary markedly between neighbourhoods.

> **Did You Know?**
> - Amsterdam's population is 735,328
> - They own 600,000 bikes
> - There are 211 coffeeshops and 86 'hash bars' (selling both soft drugs and alcohol)
> - Coffeeshops are licensed to sell 5g of marijuana to those over 18
> - Only 5% of Amsterdam's coffeeshop customers are Dutch
> - Only 10% of Dutch people own their own homes
> - The Netherlands is the world's third most densely populated country, after Bangladesh and South Korea
> - 25% of the country would be underwater if the dams burst
> - The British visit Amsterdam in the greatest numbers, followed by Americans, Germans, Italians and the Spanish

In the Netherlands' May 2002 general elections, the Christian Democratic Party was swept into power, booting the Labour party from office after 12 years in government. Its victory came after Pim Fortuyn, flamboyant leader of a right-wing populist party, was assassinated by a self-styled animal-rights activist just eight days before polling. Shocked by the murder, locals opted for conservative rule. The government has slashed welfare spending, promised to deport up to 30,000 illegal immigrants and will introduce strict reforms to disability pensions.

ECONOMY

Amsterdam has been the Netherlands' economic powerhouse since the Industrial Revolution. In the 1960s and '70s, worsening congestion and environmental issues forced many industries to seek areas with fewer constraints. However, the canal city bounced back, reinventing its role as a trade and financial services centre.

From 1980 until 2000, the Netherlands was Europe's economic miracle. According to Australian economics writer Tim Colebatch, two decades of unbroken growth expanded its economy by 50% and 'made a nation where half the population lives below sea level into one of the richest in the world' (*The Age*).

All that changed in 2002, with the country entering its first recession in 20 years. Unemployment ballooned from 2% to 6% (Amsterdam's unemployment rate hovers just under 10%).

The main economic sectors employ roughly equal numbers of people: manufacturing; commerce and finance; tourism; and science, arts and crafts. Tourism generates a turnover of almost one billion euros per year and employs 9% of the workforce.

Schiphol is Europe's fastest-growing airport and the deafening turbine noise in this built-up area is an endless source of controversy.

SOCIETY & CULTURE

Irreverently royal: queening it up on Queen's Day (Koninginnedag, p78)

The Netherlands – and Amsterdam in particular – are years ahead of the rest of the world on moral and social issues (drugs, abortion, euthanasia and homosexuality), as they believe it's pointless to try to eradicate activities such as drug use and prostitution. But the Dutch can be stunningly blunt; it seems it hardly matters how you say something, it's what you say that counts. At the same time, they also have an unusual ability to laugh at themselves and lampoon people who take themselves too seriously.

Etiquette

Amsterdammers are a pretty relaxed lot and this is reflected in their casual dress. Slightly smarter casual wear is appropriate at the theatre, opera or more upmarket restaurants; formal dress is for business and bank dealings.

The accepted greeting is a handshake. Cheek-kissing (two or three pecks) is common between people who know one another socially. If you're invited home for dinner, bring something for the host: a bunch of flowers or a plant, a bottle of wine, cake or pastries. It's polite to arrive five to 15 minutes late (never early and *definitely* no later), but business meetings start on time.

Queuing up for a Dutch delicacy: french fries with mayonnaise

QUEUING

Queue jumping is a major no-no in the Netherlands. A common convention is to pull a numbered ticket from a dispenser and wait your turn, even if there are few customers present. This applies for government offices, larger post offices, bakeries and delicatessen counters at the supermarket. Someone, if not everyone, will let you know very quickly if you've pushed in.

SMOKING

What's likely to get up the nose of nonsmoking visitors: Amsterdam establishments place few restrictions on cigarette smoking. And few will ever ask if you mind if they smoke. (See the boxed text Care for Some Food with That Smoke? on p73.) Smoking dope in some public places is frowned upon. At coffeeshops and some bars (ask the bartender) it's OK, but even the hippest locals detest foreigners who think they can toke on a joint anywhere they want. Ask first.

ARTS

Almost since its founding Amsterdam has been a major trendsetting centre of the arts. It lacked a powerful court and wealthy church, but compensated with a large middle class that didn't mind spending money on art. So it comes as little surprise that Amsterdam's international renown lies chiefly in painting and architecture.

Bonkers for Brad

In May 2004, Amsterdam was caught in the thrall of Brad Pitt, in town with George Clooney for 12 weeks – during which vast swathes of the city were shut down each night to shoot *Ocean's 12*, sequel to the blockbuster *Ocean's 11*.

Newspapers ran columns pondering whether Brad and Jen had bought a house in Jordaan, paparazzi and teenage girls alike staked out the Amstel InterContinental where Brad and George were staying, and hundreds volunteered for duties as extras. Expect increased notoriety for Amsterdam as a film venue as a result.

Art & Architecture

Most people associate Dutch art with Golden Age painters such as Rembrandt, Vermeer and Frans Hals. Amsterdam also has a wealth of works by Flemish masters such as Pieter Bruegel and Hieronymus Bosch, as the entire region was once part of the Low Countries. Other local legends include Jacob van Ruysdael, Albert Cuyp, Jan Steen, Cornelis Troost and Jacob de Wit. The tragic 19th-century Dutch master Vincent van Gogh is probably the most famous painter of all time (p9).

In the modern era, the works of visual wizards such as Piet Mondrian, HP Berlage and MC Escher help to uphold Amsterdam's reputation for innovative painting, architecture and graphic arts respectively, while the postmodern period is taken care of by architect and influential theorist Rem Koolhaas.

Music

Amsterdam has contributed little to the world's musical and theatrical heritage, but the promotion of cultural events in a city this size is unparalleled. The Concertgebouw (p92) prides itself on a world-class symphony orchestra, and top local and international talents headline in the local music clubs. A handful of pop groups with a wide following hails from here, although it's been decades since names such as Golden Earring, Shocking Blue or Jan Akkerman (guitarist for the progressive rock band Focus) first shot to fame in the late 1960s and early '70s.

The city once had a lively punk-music scene but, after a flirtation with guitar-driven rock bands in the '80s, it has evolved into a centre for house, techno and R&B. 'Gabber', Dutch dance music, is a techno-like, synthesizer-heavy genre in which the number of beats per minute is beyond belief. The city also boasts fantastic hip-hop, ska and world-music scenes.

Doing it live: Dutch pop band Di-rect at Paradiso (p87)

Directory

A flower-powered three-wheeler

MARTIN MOOS

ARRIVAL & DEPARTURE
Air

Amsterdam's Schiphol International Airport (6, E3) is highly efficient; it has to be because it handles a staggering 31 million passengers a year. The only airport in the world built on the site of a major naval battle, it is 18km southwest of the city centre. The arrivals area is on the ground floor in the Schiphol Plaza; take a left out of the passenger area to visit the **Holland Tourist Information office** (🕃 7am-10pm). The departure hall is upstairs; tax-free shopping here is great value.

INFORMATION

For airport and flight information, call ☎ 0900-01 41 (€0.10 per minute) or check www.schiphol.nl. The P1 and P2 short-term parking garages charge €3 for the first three hours and €2 for every 30 minutes thereafter. The open-air P3 long-term parking area is a fair way from the terminal but linked by a 24-hour shuttle bus; parking costs €40 for the first three days (minimum charge) and €4.50 per day thereafter.

AIRPORT ACCESS
Train

From 6am to midnight, trains run to Centraal Station every 15 minutes. The service takes 15 to 20 minutes and costs €3.50/6 one way/return. Pay with cash or by credit card.

Bus

There's an airport shuttle bus, **Connexion** (www.airporthotelshuttle .nl), that will drop you at your hotel door. It costs €10.50/19 one way/return, and leaves from platform A7 every 15 minutes from 7am to 9pm daily.

Taxi

A taxi to the city centre takes 20 to 30 minutes (longer in rush hour) and costs about €35 to €45.

Train

Amsterdam's main train station, Centraal Station, has regular and efficient connections to most destinations within the Netherlands and in neighbouring countries. International train information and reservations can be found at the **NS International Reservations Office** (Centraal Station; www. ns.nl; 🕃 7am-10pm) – expect a long wait. For information only, call the less reliable **Teleservice NS Internationaal** (☎ 0900-92 96; per min €0.40). Reserve international seats in advance in peak periods (although you can buy tickets to neighbouring countries at the normal ticket counters). For travel within Holland, just turn up at the station; you'll rarely have to wait more than an hour for a train.

Bus

The most extensive European bus network is **Eurolines** (2, C5; ☎ 560 87 87; www.eurolines.com; Rokin 10), near Dam Square. You can buy tickets at most travel agencies and at the Netherlands Railways Reisburo, Centraal Station. Buses leave from the **Eurolines bus station** (1, E5; ☎ 694 56 31) next to Amstelstation; give yourself 30 minutes to get there from Centraal Station on the metro (it's five stops away).

Boat

Services between Holland and the UK (as well as some Scandinavian routes) are run by **Stenaline** (☎ 0990-70 70 70; www.stenaline .com); **P&O North Sea Ferries** (☎ 01482-377 177; www.ponsf .com); and **DFDS Scandinavian Seaways** (☎ 0990-333 111; www .dfdsseaways.co.uk). Ask for train–boat–train deals.

Travel Documents
PASSPORT

If you're from outside the EU, you must have a passport valid for three months from the date of entry. EU citizens must have a passport or an identity card.

VISA

Visas are not required by EU citizens or by nationals of Australia, Canada, Israel, Japan, South Korea, New Zealand, Singapore and the USA. Nationals of other countries should check with their local Dutch embassy.

Customs & Duty-Free

For visitors from EU countries, ceilings only still apply for perfumes and other luxury products. Residents of non-EU European countries can bring in up to 200 cigarettes or 250g (8oz) of tobacco, 2L of wine plus 1L of spirits, 60ml of perfume, and any other goods up to the value of €167. EU citizens can bring in limitless amounts of goods, so long as they're for personal use.

Departure Tax

Departure tax is prepaid, as it's included in the price of your ticket.

Left Luggage

There is a left-luggage counter in the basement at Schiphol airport; up to 30kg can be left at the staffed counter (€6 per item per day). Left luggage at Centraal Station costs €5 per item for 24 hours.

GETTING AROUND

You can reach most places in Amsterdam on foot, but there's also an efficient public transport system combining tram, bus and metro. However, the canal belt can present minor problems as trams and buses stick to the spoke roads. Luckily, you rarely need walk more than 1km from a tram or bus stop to your destination.

Most trams and buses converge at Centraal Station. The GVB (Gemeentevervoerbedrijf or Municipal Transport Company) **information**

office (2, E2; ⊙ 7am-9pm Mon-Fri, to 7pm late Oct-Mar, from 8am Sat & Sun), in front of the station, sells tickets and passes. Pick up a free *Tourist Guide to Public Transport* booklet and transport map. For transport information, call ☎ 0900-92 92 from 6am to midnight Monday to Friday, from 7am weekends (€0.40 per minute).

Tickets & Travel Passes

Don't travel without a ticket: the Dutch love enforcing their rules, and uniformed and plain-clothes inspectors are everywhere. You'll have to pay an on-the-spot fine of €29.40, and the hard-as-nails transit police won't listen to any excuse.

Instead, buy the handy *strippenkaart* (strip card) from tobacco shops, post offices, train station counters and ticketing machines, many bookshops and newsagents, and outlets of the GVB. It's valid on all buses, trams and metros (but Schiphol Airport is not included). It costs €1.60/6.40/18.30 for 2/15/45 strips (children under four travel free, and those up to 11 pay reduced fares) and the minimum you'll use for each journey is two strips.

It works this way: Amsterdam is divided into five zones (all of the main attractions are in zone one, called Centrum). When you get on a tram, bus or train, you stamp one strip for your journey and one strip for each zone you travel in. If you're travelling in zone one only, you stamp one strip for your journey and one for the zone. If travelling in two zones, you stamp one for your journey and two for the two zones, and so on.

Stamped tickets are valid for one hour. Any number of people can travel on one *strippenkaart*, but the correct number of strips must be stamped. So if two of you are making a short journey within Centrum, you must stamp four strips.

If you're going to use a lot of public transport in one day, get a *dagkaarten* (day card), which gives adults/children unlimited travel for €6.30/4.20. Two days is €10/6.70 and three €13/8.60. (See also p116 for information on combined transport and museum passes.)

Tram

Amsterdam trams are wonderful: fast, efficient and frequent. In the past two years, conductors have been reintroduced on many routes to stop fare evasion and to increase passenger security, so you may have to enter through the rear door, where a conductor will stamp your ticket or sell you one. Exit via any door. There are also *sneltram* (light rail) lines, such as the express one out to IJburg (which opened in October 2004). Most tram lines stop running around midnight.

Bicycle

Cycling around Amsterdam is one of the joys of the Western world: riding along a canal on a sunny day is hard to beat. And, on a bike, you can get from one side of the city to the other in a few minutes. **Holland Rent-A-Bike** (2, C4; ☎ 622 32 07; Damrak 247), below Beurs van Berlage, has impeccably tuned, non-touristy-looking bikes with reliable locks for €6.50/34.50 per day/week, as does **Bike City** (5, C2; ☎ 626 37 21; Bloemgracht 68-70), for €6.75/38.50. Prices are for coaster-brake (not handbrake) bikes; expect to either leave a credit-card imprint or pay a €100 deposit. There is a strictly enforced €25 fine for riding through busy Leidsestraat (5, C6) at any time of day or night.

Bus

Buses are the best option for getting to/from the outer suburbs. Board through the front door and show your ticket to the driver. Half-hourly night buses start shortly after midnight, and run until 5am Monday to Friday (to 6.30am on weekends).

Metro

Chances are you won't use the metro unless you go to the international bus station at Amstelstation (1, E5) or south to the RAI Convention Centre (1, D5) or the World Trade Centre (1, C5). The metro stops running around midnight.

Ferry

There's a free ferry, marked 'Buiksloterwegveer', running over the IJ to north Amsterdam. It departs from between piers 8 and 9 (2, E1) behind the Centraal Station and runs every five minutes from 6.30am to 9pm, or every 10 minutes from 9pm to 6.30am. The trip takes seven minutes and carries pedestrians and bicycles, though there's not much to do when you arrive.

Canal Boat

The **Lovers Museum Boat** (☎ 622 21 81) leaves every 30 minutes from the terminal on Prins Hendrikkade (2, D2; opposite No 26, near Centraal Station) stopping at all major museums. A day ticket for unlimited travel costs €15, and provides 10% to 50% off at most museums along the route.

The **Canal Bus** (☎ 623 98 86) does a circuit of the tourist centres between Centraal Station and the Rijksmuseum from 10.15am to 6.45pm. A day pass costs €15. Canal 'bikes' (paddleboats, ☎ 626 55 74) can be hired from kiosks at Leidseplein, Keizersgracht/Leidsestraat, the Anne Frank Huis and the Rijksmuseum; two- and four-seaters cost €7/hour.

Taxi

Flag fall is €2.90, plus €1.80/km. A 5% to 10% tip is also expected if service has been fine. To call a taxi, dial ☎ 677 77 77; there's no extra cost for phone booking. In theory you must board taxis at taxi stands dotted round the city (Centraal Station, Rembrandtplein and Leidseplein are the biggest), but many will stop if hailed in the street.

Wheelchair users can phone ☎ 633 39 43 from 9am to 5pm Monday to Friday to book a wheelchair taxi.

Car & Motorcycle

Driving on Amsterdam's narrow canalside streets can be a nightmare: parking is expensive, the one-way systems Byzantine and unloading trucks often block the way. Cars with foreign plates risk being broken into, and illegally parked vehicles will be clamped, with a hefty fine attached.

At most you'll need a car for excursions outside Amsterdam. The rental market is competitive (from €35/day). The main companies include **Avis** (☎ 644 36 84), **Budget** (☎ 612 60 66) and **Europcar** (☎ 683 21 23).

Speed limits are 50km/h in built-up areas, 80km/h in the country, 100km/h on major through roads and 100km/h to 120km/h on freeways (always clearly indicated). The blood-alcohol limit is 0.05%. Drive on the right.

PRACTICALITIES
Business Hours

Most banks and businesses are closed on public holidays. Many shops open on Good Friday and on Christmas and Boxing days. Venues normally closed on Sunday are also likely to be closed on public holidays.

Banks 9am to 4pm Monday to Friday, some till 9pm Thursday and Saturday mornings.
Offices 8.30am-5pm Monday to Friday.
Post Offices 9am to 6pm Monday to Friday (to 8pm Thursday), 10am to 3pm Saturday.

Restaurants Dutch restaurants open early (around 5.30pm) and most kitchens close by 10pm.
Shops Noon-6pm Monday, 9am-6pm Tuesday to Saturday.
Pharmacies Usually 8.30am-5.30pm Monday to Friday.
Late-Night Shopping To 9pm Thursday at all larger stores and most smaller stores.

Climate & When to Go

Amsterdam is at its best from May (when the tulips are out) to August (when the days are longest). Accommodation is cheaper from November to December and can fall to ludicrously low levels in the bigger hotels in January and February. From December to March there is plenty of wind and horizontal rain.

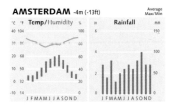

Disabled Travellers

Most offices, museums and train and metro stations have lifts and/or ramps and toilets for the disabled. However, many budget and mid-range hotels are in old buildings with steep stairs and no lifts. In addition, the cobbled streets can present problems for wheelchairs. The disabled get discounts on public transport, and can park free in designated spots (if they have the appropriate windscreen marker).

INFORMATION & ORGANISATIONS

The **Nederlands Instituut voor Zorg & Welzijn** (NIZW; ☎ 030-230 66 03; Postbus 19152, 3501 DD Utrecht), has information on accessible places to stay as well as referrals to more specific organisations. Log on to www.access-able.com for more information.

Discounts
STUDENT & YOUTH CARDS

The International Student Identity Card (ISIC), the Federation of International Youth Travel Organisations (FIYTO) card or the Euro26 card won't earn entry discounts, but are good for reductions on air and ferry tickets. GWK currency exchange (p119) offers 25% off commission to these cardholders.

For sightseers under 27, the Cultureel Jongeren Passport (CJP/CYP; Cultural Youth Pass) offers huge discounts to major museums and many cultural events. It costs €11 per year from the VVV or Amsterdam Uit Buro office (see p121).

SENIORS' CARDS

The minimum age for senior discounts is 65 (60 for partners). They apply to public transport, museum admission, theatres, concerts and more. Your home-country senior card should be proof enough, but carry a passport or identity card just in case.

CULTURAL DISCOUNT CARDS

The **Museumjaarkaart** (p7; €25/12.50 for those over 25/under 25) gives free admission to many of the highlights listed in the Highlights chapter (p8), and 400 other museums and galleries, as well as discounts to many venues; it's valid for one year and you'll need a passport photo.

If you'll be using public transport, an **Amsterdam Pass** (one/two/three days €31/41/51) gets you into all of the big galleries and museums, and includes bus, tram and train journeys and a free trip on a canal boat. It also gives discounts to some restaurants. Both cards are available from the VVV and AUB (see p121).

Electricity

If you need an adapter, try to get it at home first because most of those sold in the Netherlands are for locals going abroad.

Voltage	220V
Frequency	50 Hz
Cycle	AC
Plugs	standard continental two round pins

Embassies & Consulates

Amsterdam may be the country's capital but the government and ministries are based in The Hague, so that's where the embassies are. There are, however, many consulates in Amsterdam.

Canada (☎ 070-311 16 00; Sophialaan 7, The Hague)
UK (1, C4; ☎ 676 43 43; Koningslaan 44, Amsterdam)
USA (3, B3; ☎ 575 53 09; Museumplein 19, Amsterdam)

Emergencies

In a life-threatening emergency, the national telephone number for ambulance, police and the fire brigade is ☎ 112. For non-emergency police matters, phone ☎ 622 22 22. The Rape Crisis Line is ☎ 613 02 45. The AIDS Helpline is ☎ 0800-022 22 20 and operates from 2pm to 10pm Monday to Friday.

SAFETY CONCERNS

Amsterdam is pretty safe despite the commercial sex and soft drugs. All the same, take special care at night in the red-light district, and in crowded areas such as Centraal Station, Damrak or Leidseplein, where pickpockets operate. The most likely crime you could face is having your bicycle stolen, if you've hired one. Always – *always*, no matter how short a time you're taking your eyes off it – lock up your bicycle with a good lock. And when crossing the street, look for speeding bikes as well as cars.

Fitness
SWIMMING
The city's fanciest indoor swimming complex is Mirandabad (p39). Nearly as good is the **Marnixbad** (5, B1; ☎ 625 48 43; Marnixplein 5-9; ⏱ 10am-4pm Mon-Sat), which charges €2.25 a swim. Ring ahead for evening times. For steamy delights try **Sauna Deco** (2, B3; ☎ 623 82 15; Herengracht 115; admission €15.50, or €12.50 noon-3pm Mon-Fri), a classy Art Deco Scandinavian-style unisex sauna – not a gay venue.

GYMS
You'll find good apparatus at **Barry's Fitness Centre** (3, D3; ☎ 626 10 36; Lijnbaansgracht 350; per day €12). **A Bigger Splash** (5, C5; ☎ 624 84 04; Looiersgracht 26-30; per day/week €16/40) offers aerobics, massage and weight training.

Gay & Lesbian Travellers
Some estimates put Amsterdam's gay and lesbian population at 30%. The Netherlands allows same-sex marriages and the age of homosexual consent is 16. Gay and lesbian venues tend to be very visible and welcoming to visitors (see p95); the city even has its own Homomonument (see p23).

INFORMATION & ORGANISATIONS
The government-subsidised **COC Amsterdam** (5, C3; ☎ 623 40 79; www.cocamsterdam.nl; Rozenstraat 14) is one of the world's largest gay and lesbian rights organisations. There's also a **Gay & Lesbian Switchboard** (☎ 623 65 65; ⏱ 2-10pm).

Health
No immunisations are needed to visit the Netherlands. Tap water in Amsterdam is safe to drink. Condoms are readily available in pharmacies and supermarkets.

MEDICAL SERVICES
Travel insurance is advisable to cover any medical treatment you may need while in Amsterdam. However, the Netherlands has reciprocal medical schemes with other EU countries and Australia; check with your public health insurer to find out which form to take along. If you have to pay on the spot you'll be able to claim back home. Citizens from other countries should ensure that they have complete travel/medical insurance coverage.

Call ☎ 592 34 34 or 0900-503 20 42 (24 hours) for Centraal Doktordienst, an English-speaking service with advice on medical symptoms. For less urgent medical matters contact **GG&GD** (Municipal Medical & Health Service; 2, D7; ☎ 555 58 22; Groenburgwal 44).

Hospitals with 24-hour emergency units include:
Onze Lieve Vrouwe Gasthuis (1, E4; ☎ 599 91 11; Eerste Oosterparkstraat 1; tram 9, 14 or bus 59, 120, 126)
Sint Lucas Ziekenhuis (1, B3; ☎ 510 89 11; Jan Tooropstraat 164; tram 13, bus 19, 64 or train to Station de Vluchtlaan)
Slotervaart Ziekenhuis (1, A5; ☎ 512 41 13; Louwesweg 6)

DENTAL SERVICES
If you chip a tooth or require 24-hour emergency treatment, ring the **Dentists' Referral Agency** (☎ 570 95 95), or call the dentist administration bureau (☎ 0900-821 2230). You might be able to get into **Atlas Tandheelkundige Kliniek** (Atlas Dental Clinic; 2, F4; ☎ 622 44 62; Prins Hendrikkade 149), near the Centraal Station, at short notice.

PHARMACIES
The local *drogist* (pharmacist) can fill prescriptions or deal with minor health concerns. Dutch speakers

can ring ☎ 694 87 09 for a recorded list of 24-hour chemists; otherwise check newspapers or notices in pharmacy windows. **Dam Apotheek** (2, C5; ☎ 624 43 31; Damstraat 2; ⌚ 8.30am-6pm Mon-Fri, to 5pm Sat), is off Dam Square.

Holidays

Nieuwjaarsdag (New Year's Day) 1 January

Goede Vrijdag (Good Friday) March/ April

Eerste and Tweede Paasdag (Easter Sunday and Monday) March/ April

Koninginnedag (Queen's Day) 30 April

Hemelvaartsdag (Ascension Day) mid- to late May

Eerste and Tweede Pinksterdag (Whit Sunday and Monday) late May/ early June

Eerste and Tweede Kerstdag (Christmas Day and Boxing Day) 25 and 26 December

Internet

If you packed your laptop, note that Holland uses a four-pin phone plug that accommodates a US, French or Australian-style jack but not the six-pin UK model. Adapters are best brought from home.

INTERNET CAFÉS

There are plenty of Internet cafés dotted around town, including:
easyEverything (www.easyevery thing.com; 2, C8; Reguliersbreestraat 22; per hr €1-3; ⌚ 10am-8pm, to 10pm in summer) Also at Damrak 33 (2, D3) and Leidsestraat 24 (2, A8).
Freeworld (www.freeworld-internet cafe.nl; Nieuwendijk 30; per 30min €1; ⌚ 9am-1am Sun-Thu, to 3am Fri & Sat).

USEFUL WEBSITES

Lonely Planet's website (www.lonely planet.com) offers a speedy link to many Dutch websites. Others (in English) include:

Amsterdam Virtual Tour (www.channels.nl)
City of Amsterdam (www.amsterdam.nl)
Special Bite (www.specialbite.nl) Restaurant guide.
Underwater Amsterdam (www .underwateramsterdam.com) An alternative listings guide.

Lost Property

GVB info office (2, E2; ☎ 551 49 11; Prins Hendrikkade 108-114; ⌚ 9.30am-4.30pm Mon-Fri) For items found on buses, trams or the metro.
Gevonden Voor werpen (Lost & Found office; ☎ 557 85 44; ⌚ 24hr) At Centraal Station near the luggage lockers; for items left on trains.
Police lost-property office (1, E4; ☎ 559 30 05; Stephensonstraat 18; ⌚ 9.30am-3.30pm Mon-Fri)

Metric System

The metric system is standard. Staff in many shops refer to 100g as an *ons* and 500g as a *pond*. Technically, the use of *ons* is forbidden but it's an ingrained habit. Like other Continental Europeans, the Dutch use commas in decimals, and points to indicate thousands. See the conversion table below.

TEMPERATURE
°C = (°F - 32) ÷ 1.8
°F = (°C x 1.8) + 32

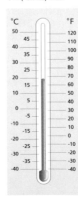

DISTANCE
1in = 2.54cm
1cm = 0.39in
1m = 3.3ft = 1.1yd
1ft = 0.3m
1km = 0.62 miles
1 mile = 1.6km

WEIGHT
1kg = 2.2lb
1lb = 0.45kg
1g = 0.04oz
1oz = 28g

VOLUME
1L = 0.26 US gallons
1 US gallon = 3.8L
1L = 0.22 imperial gallons
1 imperial gallon = 4.55L

Money

ATMS

ATMs are found outside most banks, in the airport halls and in the main hall of Centraal Station.

CHANGING MONEY

Avoid the private exchange booths dotted along Rokin and the Damrak: they're convenient and open late hours but commissions and rates are lousy. Banks and post offices offer official exchange rates with €1 to €2 commission, as do the **Grenswisselkantoren** (GWK, Border Exchange Offices; ☎ 0800-566; free service), with 24-hour offices at Centraal Station and Schiphol.

CREDIT CARDS

All major cards are recognised, but Amsterdam is still strongly cash based and many smaller places, especially restaurants and bars, may refuse card payment or levy a surcharge. Report lost or stolen cards on these 24-hour numbers:
American Express (☎ 504 80 00 9am-6pm Mon-Fri, ☎ 504 86 66 at other times)
Diners Club (☎ 654 55 11)
MasterCard/Eurocard (☎ 030-283 55 55; Utrecht)
Visa (☎ 0800-02 31 10)

CURRENCY

The local currency is the euro. It comes in €200, €100, €50, €20, €10 and €5 notes, as well as the rarely spotted €500 note. There are also €2 and €1 coins, as well as various smaller coinage. One euro is made up of 100 cents.

TRAVELLERS CHEQUES

Banks charge a commission to exchange cheques. **American Express** (2, C4; ☎ 0800-022 01 00; Damrak 66) and **Thomas Cook** (2, C5; ☎ 0800-022 86 30 or 625 09 22 for lost/stolen cheques; Dam 23-25 or Leidseplein 31A) do not. Shops, restaurants and hotels prefer cash.

Newspapers & Magazines

The European editions of the *Economist* and *Time* are printed here, and European editions of English newspapers such as the *Guardian* and the *Independent* are available at most newsstands. The largest Dutch-language newspaper is *De Telegraaf*, a right-wing sensationalist daily. *De Volkskrant* is a one-time Catholic daily with leftist leanings, and *Het Parool* is an Amsterdam evening paper. Its daily PS supplement with a what's-on listing on Saturday can be useful even if you don't read Dutch.

Photography & Video

Expect to pay €5 or more for a good-quality 36-exposure film. Developing will cost about €7 per roll. The **Kruidvat shop** (Kalverstraat 187) is good or, for professional same-day developing, try **Kleurgamma** (☎ 665 53 01; Mauritskade 55), just southeast of the canal belt.

Like most of Europe and Australia, the Netherlands uses the PAL system, which is incompatible with the American and Japanese NTSC system.

Post

Stamps are sold at post-office counters and some newsagents, hotels and museums. Use the mailbox slits marked Overige Postcodes (Other Postal Codes) if you don't hand mail in at a counter. Call ☎ 0800-04 17 for general postal inquiries between 8am and 8pm Monday to Friday. The well-equipped main post office is at Singel 250 (2, A5). You can have mail sent to you there at poste restante, Hoofdpostkantoor PTT, Singel 250, 1012 SJ Amsterdam.

POSTAL RATES

Letters up to 20g posted priority within Europe cost €0.55. Beyond

Europe, letters cost €0.87 priority. Postcards to anywhere outside the Netherlands cost €0.77 (priority only).

Radio

Dutch radio offers a mix of programs as eclectic as you'll find anywhere. The BBC World Service broadcasts on 648kHz medium wave, and has occasional news programs in German. Other stations you can pick up include the following:

BBC Radio 4 (198kHz FM) News and drama
BBC Radio 5 (693kHz FM) Sports
Radio Hondert (98.3kHz FM) Eclectic mix of world music; biggest independent Amsterdam station
Radio de Vrije Keyser (96.2kHz FM) Politics, punk music and squat news (for the best squats in town)

Telephone

There are plenty of public phones, but most accept national phonecards only (the cheapest card is €5). Some take credit cards but few accept coins, especially since the conversion to the euro. Calls cost €0.30 per minute.

PHONECARDS

Post offices and newsagencies sell a wide range of local and international phonecards.

MOBILE PHONES

The Netherlands uses the GSM cellular phone system, compatible with phones sold in the UK, Australia and most of Asia, but not those from North America or Japan. Before you leave home, check that your service provider has a roaming agreement with a local counterpart.

COUNTRY & CITY CODES

The country code for the Netherlands is ☎ 31; Amsterdam's area code is ☎ 20.

USEFUL PHONE NUMBERS

Local directory inquiries	☎ 0900-80 08
International directory inquiries	☎ 0900-84 18
Operator	☎ 0800-04 10
Reverse-charge (collect)	☎ 0800-01 01

Television

Dutch TV is generally a great cure for insomnia, but there is also a large number of ad-free, English-language sitcoms and films with Dutch subtitles. BBC1 and BBC2 are available on cable. You'll also find channels from Belgium, France, Germany, Italy and Spain, Euro-channels with sports and music clips, and of course CNN. Also check the Teletext pages behind many TV channels for pages of news, weather, aircraft departure times at Schiphol airport and more.

Time

The Netherlands is on Central European Time (GMT plus one hour). Clocks are put forward one hour for daylight saving at 2am on the last Sunday in March and go back at 3am on the last Sunday in October.

Tipping

Tipping isn't compulsory, but most people add 5% to 10% in taxis if service has been fine. In restaurants, there's a service charge included; people will round up the total to the nearest euro for smaller bills, and to the nearest €5 for a large bill. A tip of 10% is considered generous. In pubs with outdoor or table service, you can just leave small change on the table. Toilet attendants expect €0.25 to €0.50, although €1 is the rule in some clubs.

Toilets

Bars and department stores or other places handy to pop into to use the toilet – but be prepared to pay at least

€0.25 for the pleasure. But at least these toilets are generally spotless (if not, you should complain).

Tourist Information

Though always busy, the main tourist information source, the VVV (Vereniging voor Vreemdelingen-Verkeer – literally, Society for Foreigner Traffic), is a delight. It sells maps, discount passes and theatre tickets, books hotel rooms at no cost and answers tourist inquiries. The **GWK currency-exchange office** (☎ 627 27 27, ☻ 7.45am-10pm) inside Centraal Station also books hotel rooms and is less crowded than the VVV offices.

The VVV has four offices: a busy one in front of **Centraal Station** (2, E2; Stationsplein 10; ☻ hotel bookings 9am-5pm, transport & ticket information 7am-9pm Mon-Fri, 8am-9pm Sat & Sun); **inside Centraal Station** (Platform 2a; ☻ 8am-7.45pm Mon-Sat, 9am-5pm Sun); and **Leidseplein** (5, C6; Leidseplein 1; ☻ 9am-7pm Mon-Fri, to 5pm Sat & Sun). **Holland Tourist Information** (☻ 7am-10pm), also VVV, is at Schiphol airport. VVV staff also field phone queries in Dutch, English and German on ☎ 0900-400 40 40 (€1.20 per minute), 9am to 5pm Monday to Friday.

AMSTERDAM UIT BURO

For anything related to entertainment, head to the **Amsterdam Uit Buro** (AUB; 5, C6; ☎ 488 77 78 Leidseplein 26; ☻ 10am-6pm, to 9pm Thu), which has free brochures and sells tickets (with a €1.50 mark-up). Its phone service **Uitlijn** (☎ 0900-01 91, aub@aub.nl; per min €0.40) operates from 9am to 9pm. For bookings from abroad, call the **National Reservations Centre** (☎ +31-70-320 25 00).

Women Travellers

Amsterdam is about as safe as it gets among Europe's major cities, and there's little street harassment. Dutch women are a confident lot and are generally treated accordingly. However, at night in the red-light district, you might get some unwelcome attention if walking by yourself.

LANGUAGE

Almost every Amsterdammer speaks English. Nonetheless, a few words in Dutch show goodwill, which is always appreciated, and you'll begin to understand more of what's going on.

Basics

Hello.	*Dag/Hallo*
Goodbye.	*Dag*
See you (again).	*Tot ziens*
Yes/No.	*Ja/Nee*
Please.	*Alstublieft/ Al sjeblieft (polite/informal)*
Thank you.	*Dank u/ Bedankt*
You're welcome.	*Geen dank*
Excuse me.	*Pardon*
I (don't) understand.	*Ik begrijp het (niet)*
Do you speak English?	*Spreekt u Engels?*
Please write it down.	*Schrijf het alstublieft*
How are you?	*Hoe gaat het met (u/jou)?*
I'm fine, thanks.	*Goed, bedankt*
What's your name?	*Hoe heet u? (polite) Hoe heet je? (informal)*
My name is ...	*Ik heet ...*
Where are you from?	*Waar komt u vandaan? (polite) Waar kom je vandaan? (informal)*
I'm from ...	*Ik kom uit ...*
Do you have (a) ...?	*Heeft u (een) ...?*
How much is it?	*Hoeveel is het?*
Help!	*Help!*

Accommodation

camping ground	*camping*
guesthouse	*pension*
hotel	*hotel*
youth hostel	*jeugdherberg*

Do you have any rooms available?	*Heeft u kamers vrij?*
How much is it per night/ per person?	*Hoeveel is het per nacht/ per persoon?*
Is breakfast included?	*Is het ontbijt inbegrepen?*
May I see the room?	*Mag ik de kamer zien?*

Getting Around

Where is the ...?	*Waar is ...?*
bus stop	*de bushalte*
metro station	*het metrostation*
train station	*het treinstation*
tram stop	*de tramhalte*
What time does the ... leave?	*Hoe laat vertrekt de ...?*
What time does the ... arrive?	*Hoe laat komt de ... aan?*
bus	*bus*
train	*trein*
tram	*tram*
What street/ road is this?	*Welke straat/ weg is dit?*
How do I get to ...?	*Hoe kom ik bij ...?*

Waar is de tram?

(Go) straight ahead.	*(Ga) rechtdoor*
left/right	*links/rechts*

Around Town

Where is a/the ...?	*Waar is ...?*
public toilet	*een openbaar toilet*
post office	*het postkantoor*
tourist office	*de VVV*

Days & Time

Monday	Maandag
Tuesday	Dinsdag
Wednesday	Woensdag
Thursday	Donderdag
Friday	Vrijdag
Saturday	Zaterdag
Sunday	Zondag

What time is it?	Hoe laat is het?
When?	Wanneer?
today	vandaag
yesterday	gisteren
tomorrow	morgen

Numbers

0	nul
1	één
2	twee
3	drie
4	vier
5	vijf
6	zes
7	zeven
8	acht
9	negen
10	tien
11	elf
12	twaalf
13	dertien
14	viertien
15	vijftien
16	zestien
17	zeventien
18	achttien
19	negentien
20	twintig
100	honderd
1000	duizend
one million	miljoen

Index

See also separate indexes for Eating (p125), Sleeping (p126), Shopping (p126) and Sights with map references (p127).

EATING

SLEEPING

SHOPPING

Sights Index

FEATURES

Puccini	*Eating*
Muziektheater	*Entertainment*
Blincker	*Drinking*
Siberie	*Café*
Van Gogh Museum	*Highlights*
Bijenkorf	*Shopping*
Tram Museum	*Sights/Activities*
The Grand	*Sleeping*

AREAS

	Beach, Desert
	Building
	Land
	Mall
	Other Area
	Park/Cemetary
	Sports
	Urban

HYDROGRAPHY

	River, Creek
	Intermittent River
	Canal
	Swamp
	Water

BOUNDARIES

	State, Provincial
	Regional, Suburb
	Ancient Wall

ROUTES

	Tollway
	Freeway
	Primary Road
	Secondary Road
	Tertiary Road
	Lane
	Under Construction
	One-Way Street
	Unsealed Road
	Mall/Steps
	Tunnel
	Walking Path
	Walking Trail
	Track
	Walking Tour

TRANSPORT

	Airport, Airfield
	Bus Route
	Cycling, Bicycle Path
	Ferry
	General Transport
	Metro
	Monorail
	Rail
	Taxi Rank
	Tram

SYMBOLS

	Bank, ATM
	Buddhist
	Castle, Fortress
	Christian
	Diving, Snorkeling
	Embassy, Consulate
	Hospital, Clinic
	Information
	Internet Access
	Islamic
	Jewish
	Lighthouse
	Lookout
	Monument
	Mountain, Volcano
	National Park
	Parking Area
	Petrol Station
	Picnic Area
	Point of Interest
	Police Station
	Post Office
	Swimming Pool
	Telephone
	Toilets
	Zoo, Bird Sanctuary
	Waterfall